# TO
# THE
# CROWDS
# IN
# PARABLES

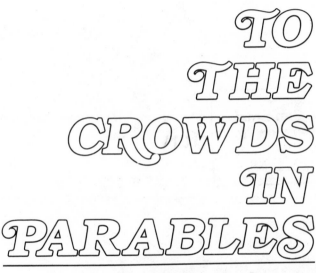

# TO THE CROWDS IN PARABLES

**G. William Jones**

**Argus Communications** · A Division of DLM, Inc.
Allen, Texas 75002 U.S.A.

Cover photo: Norman Myers/BRUCE COLEMAN

The Bible Text in this publication is from the Today's English Version Bible—New Testament: Copyright © American Bible Society, 1966, 1971, 1976. Used by permission.

**Argus Communications**
A Division of DLM, Inc.
One DLM Park
Allen, Texas 75002 U.S.A.

International Standard Book Number 0-89505-064-1
Library of Congress Number 81-69699

0 9 8 7 6 5 4 3 2 1

# CONTENTS

# Introduction

"I'm going to tell you a story."

From our earliest years, we have heard these words with excitement, anticipation, and—usually—relief.

In sickness, they meant that we were going to be able to forget about ourselves for a while, about our aches and pains, and be carried away by our imaginations.

In school, they meant that we were being offered a truce from the long periods of lecture and recitation, and that the classroom walls would soon cease to be a prison and melt away.

In lecture halls, churches, theaters—wherever people gather to look at and listen to other people—there is almost always a sudden change whenever the speaker launches into a narrative. The audience suddenly becomes quiet, forgetting even to cough, sniff, or squirm, as the tale is spun. When they understand that it is over (and that now the speaker will draw a moral, make important announcements, etc.), the change back to coughing, sniffing, and squirming is equally as sudden.

Actually, it hardly matters what kind of story it is, how good, how funny, or how moving it is, or how well it is told. There is something almost automatically captivating about a story that catches our minds and makes us forget to breathe until it is over.

If the story is short enough, that is. For we are also impatient creatures, and retain the attention span of our earliest years, becoming five- to ten-minute "dropouts" unless the story and storyteller are both of the highest quality. There is such a universal, ready-made attentiveness in most persons for short, pungent stories that it is amazing how little we use stories for the purposes of communication!

1

Teachers and preachers have much the same problem in communicating. They have from twenty to fifty minutes in which to communicate some ideas, some information, or some opinions which they hope will enlighten or motivate their audiences—or at least cause them to think. The usual tendency for coping with this problem comes much more from our Greek progenitors than from our Semitic progenitors. In order to head off all possibilities for misunderstanding, to make the message as clear as possible, we shuck it of its lifelike, experiential wrappings and lay it out as an abstract, propositional statement. As professional observers and students of life and the world, teachers and preachers tend to think of their role as one of predigestion. Much as the mother Eskimo chews up food and then transfers it to the toothless mouth of her baby, school and church communicators observe actual occurrences and experiences, extract from them their "kernel of truth," then turn to give their hearers only the bare kernel, shed of its confusing trappings. The prejudice seems to be that a straightforward $A + B = C$ approach is the clearest and therefore most understandable and meaningful form of communication from one mind to another.

## PARABLE AS ANCIENT TRADITION

Communicators who happen to be Christians are apt to think much of what Jesus had to say, but little about the *way* in which he said it.

Matthew, Mark, and Luke tell us not only *what* Jesus said when he taught the crowds and his disciples, but *how* he taught them—with parables.

> Jesus used parables to tell all these things to the crowds; he would not say a thing to them without using a parable. He did this to make come true what the prophet had said,
> "I will use parables when I speak to them;
> I will tell them things unknown since the creation
> of the world." (Matt. 13:34–35)
>
> Then the disciples came to Jesus and asked him, "Why do you use parables when you talk to the people?"
>
> Jesus answered, "The knowledge about the secrets of the Kingdom of heaven has been given to you, but not to them. For the person who has something will be given more, so that he will have more than enough; but the person who has nothing will have taken away from him even the little he has. The reason I use parables in talking to them is that they look, but

do not see, and they listen, but do not hear or understand. So the prophecy of Isaiah applies to them:

'This people will listen and listen, but not understand;
they will look and look, but not see,
because their minds are dull,
and they have stopped up their ears
and have closed their eyes.
Otherwise, their eyes would see,
their ears would hear,
their minds would understand,
and they would turn to me, says God,
and I would heal them.'

"As for you, how fortunate you are! Your eyes see and your ears hear. I assure you that many prophets and many of God's people wanted very much to see what you see, but they could not, and to hear what you hear, but they did not."

(Matt. 13:10–17)

Of course, Jesus was not the first teacher to utilize parables. They are a form of illustration found in much of the folklore of the ancient world, particularly in that of the Semitic peoples. The Old Testament abounds in parables, as does the Talmud.

The word *parable,* from the Greek *parabole,* means something like "juxtaposition for the sake of comparison." In its purest form, the parable puts forward a single point of comparison between some abstract declaration or demand and a vivid story or situation. Other characteristics of the pure parable are its self-explanatory nature and its possession of both a literal and a figurative meaning (as Jesus' parable of the mustard seed).

The Semitic parable is very different from the more Greek rhetorical form—allegory—in that an allegory contains many points of comparison within its story form, whereas a parable has only one point. In an allegory, everything stands for some abstract principle or moral, while in a parable, the whole story stands for only one principle or moral.

Another form of rhetorical address, that of the fable, has some kinship with the parable. However, the fable usually has animals for its characters, does not necessarily deal with a situation that might normally occur, and is usually satisfied with teaching a lesson on a much less lofty ethical plane than that of the parable.

So much for the place and pedigree of parable as a traditional form of public address. Perhaps the next question is, "In this modern day and age, when old forms are rapidly dropping away and being re-placed by radically new forms, why drag up such an old form as parable for modern thought and discussion?"

There are several things about parables which suit them for modern communication better, perhaps, than any other verbal form now exist-ing or soon to be developed.

## PARABLE AS IMPLICIT COMMUNICATION

If I want my listener not only to hear but also to understand, then I must give him something to do besides mere passive listening. I must give him room to work on what I am saying—to do his own share of the communicative task. If I make what I sense to be the "truth" of what I am saying as explicit as possible, then I have taken his work away from him and have done it myself. I have forced him back into the passive stance. However, if I am willing to let the "truth" in what I am saying remain implicit, then his share of the work—the interpre-tation, or making the implicit explicit—is left for him to do.

Thus, my use of the parable becomes an invitation for my listener's involvement. He may not do his explicating the way I would have done it. He may not come up with the same kernel of truth of which I was thinking when I told the parable. I take the risk that he "listens but does not understand." But there is also the possibility that, in rummaging about in the parable for himself, he may come up with a truth that is truer than my truth. At any rate, whatever he gets from the experience will be *his* truth, which he garnered for himself, and not *my* truth, to which he could give only mental assent or rejection (and neither of these possibilities is very dynamic).

## PARABLE AS CONCRETE ADDRESS

If I want to address a person about what is important in her life, it had better sound like her life to her. Abstractions *about* life may seem to me to be much neater, more precise, and more direct forms of address; but again, I may be doing too much. I may be doing her share of the understanding and learning work. For, from where do I draw my abstractions? Those I hold most dear and true I have drawn from my own experiences. In fact, I realize that the most essential learning act in my life is the act in which I take stock of many of my experiences and abstract a concept from them.

Then, just as making the implicit explicit is essentially the work of the learner and not of the teacher, so may drawing abstract conclusions from concrete experiences be essentially the work of the learner and not of the teacher.

## PARABLE AS INDIRECT COMMUNICATION

If I want to speak to a person regarding something about which he is defensive, to which he will refuse to listen once he perceives its drift, then I must communicate with him indirectly or not at all. Through indirect, roundabout means, I may pierce his defenses before he is aware that he is being addressed, or that the subject of the address is something he would rather avoid. That parable is one of the most effective forms of this type of indirect address is amply exemplified in the Old Testament story of Nathan's reproval of David for his adultery with Bathsheba and his murder of Uriah (2 Sam. 12:1–15). Afraid for his head if he approaches David directly, Nathan instead tells him a parable cast in a setting that is instantly familiar and sympathetic to David. In terms of a wealthy sheepherder stealing the one lamb of a poor sheepherder, Nathan sets up the tale. Thinking the parable to be a direct communication, David demands to be shown the man who would be so evil as to do such a thing. "You are that man!" ring the words of Nathan, who then explains that the "wealthy sheepherder" was David with many wives, while the "poor sheepherder" was Uriah with the one beloved wife, Bathsheba. Through the use of parable, Nathan enabled David to see a relationship that he had not perceived before, and thus to condemn himself, rather than be condemned.

## PARABLE AS PICTORIAL IMAGERY

Parable is not the only ancient form of communication that is today being dusted off and put back into use. The resurgence of parable is only a symptom of a much larger renewal or revolution which has taken place, roughly, within the past twenty-five years. During this time we have, subtly at first but overwhelmingly now, returned to a cultural situation in which people receive much more of their information, entertainment, and perhaps motivation through the projected image than through the printed word. It has taken a Marshall McLuhan to make us vividly aware of the fact that mass communication today is much more like it was before Gutenberg and the printing press than it

5

was just fifty years ago. Before Gutenberg, the masses relied largely upon visual images and short, simple bursts of spoken words for their information and entertainment. The advent of the printing press made printed matter cheap and available to the masses. This availability of reading matter was one of the major factors that gave rise to public education and finally to mass literacy. And mass literacy sent the communicative image into eclipse in favor of linear forms of communication. Thus, the rise of public education was accompanied by a rise in the use of linear, propositional, abstract forms of communication— a hang-up from which it has been very difficult to recover.

But in the past few years, especially since the nationwide availability of television reception, the masses are once again being informed and entertained by visual images and short, simple bursts of words. By the time the average high schooler graduates, he or she will have spent more time watching television than attending class, and will have viewed perhaps ten times more films than he or she will have read books. The television set will have been spouting images for an average of at least five hours per day, and the entire family will have spent more time watching projected visual images than they will have spent at any activity other than sleeping and working.

Into this situation reemerges the lowly parable, a form of verbal expression most suited to a visual culture. It comes closer to being "visual" than any other verbal or linear form, because it is, above all, word imagery—pictorial imagery carried through words. Like a novel, it paints its characters and settings with words upon the mind's eye of its readers or hearers. But it has the added faculty—which not even the short story can match—of being able to attract attention, paint images, bring off situations in which some truth is presented concretely and implicitly, and conclude within little more than the attention span required by a television commercial.

## WE ARE SURROUNDED BY PARABLES

The parable form is not exhausted by short, verbal narratives like those in this book. Actually, any representation of life and its concerns—if done in a dramatic, implicit, concrete, and vivid manner— can be received as parable, whether it be a painting, a play, or a motion picture.

But the final object of parable makers, I assume, is not simply to call people's attention to the parables that are all around them in various art forms. That is a worthy task certainly, but the final purpose of parable is to help people be alert for the parables that take place in their own lives. God is continually thrusting parables into the life-stream of people and nations, but

> " 'their minds are dull
> and they have stopped up their ears
> and have closed their eyes.' "

Parables are told so that

> " 'their eyes would see,
> their ears would hear,
> their minds would understand,
> and they would turn to me, says God,
> and I would heal them.' "     (Matt. 13:15)


## RESPONDING TO THE PARABLES IN THIS BOOK

As you look through this book, you will find that it has three basic components: (1) twenty-two modern parables, (2) nineteen biblical parables (or metaphors) from the Gospels, and (3) "Suggested Questions for Thought and Discussion" for each parable.

You may be using this book either as an individual or as a member of a group. If you are reading the parables in preparation for a group meeting, it is suggested that you take some time to read over and think about the questions related to each of your readings so that you may be better prepared for any discussion during your group's meeting. (Rereading as a follow-up to group meetings is also suggested.) If you are not a member of a group, you are still strongly urged to read and to ponder upon the appropriate questions as a way of getting more out of your reading experience.

This book is accompanied by a set of two audiocassettes on which all of the modern parables have been presented in a semidramatic manner. Members of groups will probably listen to the cassettes during their meetings prior to discussion. During the playing of cassettes, you are urged to follow along in your book, perhaps underlining passages that you do not understand or that you want to remark about later. Even if you are not responding to these parables as a group member, you may want a set of cassettes for private listening or for sharing with your family and friends.

The modern parables begin with one which, in addition to this Introduction, is intended to show how parables work.

# The Man
## Who Would Communicate

A young man sat in his garden. For want of anything better to do (actually it was because he was looking for any excuse for not doing what he was supposed to be doing) he looked about him. As he looked he began to notice the weeds in his garden. They were flourishing in a corner of the garden where the grass was very thin. This was the place where no fertilizer had been spread last spring, he remembered, and also where the water sprayer hardly ever reached. Staring at that patch of weeds, it suddenly struck him how strange it was that weeds flourished under exactly the opposite conditions from grass. The much more desirable grass took so much care from him in order to grow, whereas the weeds seemed to thrive under neglect.

"How like life," he thought, startled that the pattern of humanity was so closely duplicated by that which was not human. "A human life can grow without care and attention as the weed does, but that which it produces is most often undesirable. That which is desirable in human life, on the other hand, is yielded from a life into which much care and attention has been invested—like the grass!"

Excited and trembling, he grabbed pen and paper to write down the insight which he had glimpsed from the weeds and grass. In writing he tried to extract from its setting the precious seed of truth which he had seen, and to write it down in as few and as clear words as he could. Finally, after he had scratched out many words and wadded up much paper, he sank back, satisfied with a few lines upon a sheet:

*You can live without caring or being cared for and flourish for a time, but that life which produces the most helpful acts must be carefully prepared for and constantly cared for.*

As he put the paper down, his eyes wandered again around the garden. They fell upon the flower bed. How carefully he had dug all the grass and weeds from that plot, crumbling each clod between his fingers until the soil was soft and even. Then he had planted the flower seeds and fertilized them. Every day he had watered them until they grew up and bloomed. But now he saw that the tallest plant of all—the one which bore the most blooms—was not one which he had planted at all, but a weed!

"Again, how like life," he whispered to himself, startled anew. "This is another message, which corrects and develops the first!"

Quickly he took the sheet of paper upon which he had written and added these words:

*But even when the life is carefully prepared for and constantly cared for, it may produce greater evil than good unless it is critically and objectively evaluated again and again.*

The young man's heart began to beat rapidly with the enormous importance of what he felt he had discovered, and how he had discovered it.

In a fit of union with all that is, he fell to his knees on the grass, put his eye close to the earth, and strained to see as deep as he could. Then turning over on his back, he stared straight up into the sky, straining to see as far and as much as he could.

"It's all alike!" he shouted, remembering how the models of the atom he had seen looked exactly like the models of the solar system which he had also seen. "It's all the same, from the most infinitesimal to the most magnitudinous. Every truth in the universe is repeated again and again a million times, in everything that is! There is order, meaning, unity. We are surrounded by meaning. *Everything* speaks the truth to those who will see and hear!"

With the whole universe shouting the truth, he knew that he could hardly be silent himself. He did not remember ever having heard those truths which he had discovered there in the garden, and he doubted that many others had heard of them.

So when he had calmed down a bit, he went forth to teach. The eager young man taught wherever he could find several people gathered together. Calling for their attention, he would share his insights with them and tell them what he had learned about life and the world. As clearly and concisely as he could, he would spell out for them the concepts, theories, and aphorisms which he had laboriously extracted from his experiences in the garden.

The people would usually listen to him politely. But he was very disappointed that they did not begin to tremble and shake with the same excitement which had gripped him when he had first discovered those very truths.

"That's very nice," most of them would say as they walked away after he had finished, or, "I certainly enjoyed your speech."

"Do come back and speak to us again," a few of the little old ladies might tell him. "You have such a lovely voice, and we're always glad to see a young man who's really enthusiastic about something—no matter what it is."

The young man could not understand why the people could hear his words and remain so calm, so unimpressed, when he was sure that what he was telling them came hot from the seething core of the universe. It was not long until his once-precious words began to feel like ashes in his mouth when he stood up to speak before the people. He felt that his words were tumbling from his lips to fall in broken heaps at his toes, rather than rushing out to pierce the hearts and minds of his hearers.

Much disillusioned, beginning to doubt even the truth which he had discovered and embarrassed to try any longer to communicate it, the young man gave up teaching and went back to spend the days in his garden.

The grass, weeds, and flowers, the atoms and the solar systems still shouted their messages of universal truth at him, and he was often breathless with the impact of their meaning; but he despaired of being able to communicate it to anyone else. He felt that the precious gift of truth was hopelessly locked up inside of him, turning from light into a heavy mold.

"How I wish that all the people I have tried to talk to," he lamented, "could come and sit with me in this garden. We would just sit together, and I wouldn't say a word until their eyes too happened to stray to the strangely familiar way in which the grass and weeds and flowers grow, until their minds too were fired with these likenesses that fired my mind. Then we would rejoice together, and talk of what we had seen. The people would find the truth for themselves, rather than having to find it in these paltry, somehow inadequate words of mine. But alas, my garden is far too small, and the people too far away."

As he was saying this, it slowly dawned upon the young man that the way in which he had learned must be the same way in which the others had to learn. He saw that much of what had excited him about his earlier discoveries was not only the truth itself (which, after all, had been around for a long time, had been spoken by many teachers, and was in many books), but that it had become *his* truth when he had extracted it himself from his own experiences in the garden.

"What a *fool* I am!" he shouted, hitting himself on the forehead with the flat of his palm. "I have *deprived* my listeners of the very thing that gave me such joy in the truth—the act of finding and formulating it *for themselves*. I have been talking too much and taking too much upon *myself*. After learning something from a rich experience, I have taken that experience and boiled it down until there was nothing left of it but a few words, and then expected people to become as excited as I was when I handed them these miserable extracts of *words*. They need the same experience I had, or one very much like it. They need to have the opportunity, as I had, to rummage about in these experiences until they come up with the truth-extract for themselves."

The young man fell to his knees, beating his breast and moaning, "O God, forgive my arrogance! I have attempted to take thy concrete, eloquent world of experience and to boil it down into a few handy abstractions—mere concepts which I could carry about in the corner of my mouth and spit at people. And then I have had the audacity to expect them to respond with enlightenment to my words alone, when what enlightened me was thy world of experience. And more than that, I have become moody, insulted, and despondent when my words have not garnered disciples, who have understood thy truth precisely as I have understood it!"

"Henceforth," he prayed, his eyes streaming, "let me be content to be a servant of thy truth, and not pose as its master. Let me be a midwife to the birth of understanding in others, and not pose as the adoption agency!"

So saying, he rose to his feet, hitched up his breeches, and went forth again to teach. But this time, whenever he came upon a group of people, he did not attempt to instruct them with propositions, concepts, theories, and abstractions. Instead he merely recounted to them, as vividly as he could, little stories of the experiences through which he had been able to learn some truths about life and the world. He told them simple stories of grass and weeds, of atoms and solar systems, of buyers and sellers, of lovers and warriors, of farmers and merchants, in terms of things they already knew.

Some said that they heard nothing, only the wind in the trees.

Others, upon hearing him, protested, "Are we children to be told stories? Give us a mature lecture, as you used to do!"

And yet others said, "Why are you so obtuse? Tell us the truth plainly rather than beating about the bush this way. We can't make head or tail of what you say."

But there were others who, as he spoke, felt themselves transplanted into the experiences of which he spoke. Forgetting to cough or squirm, they listened spellbound to his words as their mind's eye envisioned for them the barns and palaces, stores and fields, kitchens and bedrooms of which he spoke. They found that even after he had ceased speaking, his stories continued to open doors for them into previously unrecognized meanings of their own daily experiences. They found that no matter how often they heard the stories, or thought about them, or repeated them to their children, there was always a depth within those stories which pulled people into their very fabric, inviting them to walk about, look around, and to discover things for themselves. The heretofore unseen similarities between areas of their experience, the known illuminating the unknown, taught them to look for other similarities, and to learn thereby.

Sometimes when he had finished telling a story, some of the people would want him to stay and talk with them awhile about the story. Steadfastly he refused to "tell them what the story meant," insisting that the interpretation of the story was the work of the listener. Instead he helped them to draw and create their own meanings by asking them simple questions about their reactions to the stories. The questions sometimes became levers with which the people could pry open closed doors in their minds.

"What a great teacher you are," the people said to him. "You make things plain to us which before were cloudy, vague, or unnoticed."

"No," he demurred, "it is not I who do this for you. You do it for yourselves. The only truth which you will ever really know is that which you see for yourselves."

As he turned to leave, he said over his shoulder, "I only try to help you see."

**THEME ONE**

# Mission Versus Institution

## Introduction to the Modern Parables

Isn't it strange that we so often think of the Church as a *building?* Of course, we all know that the Church is the *people,* bound together with God, with the church of the past, and with one another, through Jesus, the Christ. If we let ourselves think too much of the Church as if it were a building, or even as if it were a rather complex organization, we tend to forget that the Church exists only to serve the world, to give itself away to those who need its Word, its care. That is its mission—*our* mission.

# *The Village That Forgot*

A certain rich man was traveling one day in the country near his summer home. As his carriage passed through a small village, he was touched to notice that all the people there seemed very poor. The men and women sat listlessly in the doorways of their run-down houses, and children sat in the dust at their feet, too hungry and sick to play.

The rich man stopped his carriage and called his steward to come forward to him from another carriage behind.

"Beginning today," he told the steward, "I want you to give every man, woman, and child in this village enough money to enable them to be properly fed, clothed, doctored, and housed."

The steward bowed to his employer, then rushed to do his bidding as the rich man rode away in his carriage.

When the townsfolk heard the news, they rejoiced and praised the name of their benefactor. From that day on, no one starved or went ill-clothed or sick or homeless in that entire village.

However, several months later the rich man suffered some bad returns on his investments, and several of his businesses in the city were closed as a result. Sorrowfully, he told his steward that the amount of money he had been giving the villagers would have to be cut in half.

When the steward journeyed to the village to bring this bad news to the people, they were infuriated and nearly killed the poor man before he and his horse could outdistance the stones that were thrown at him by young and old.

A few months later, the rich man's fortunes declined even further, and the villagers' dole had to be cut again. Upon hearing this news, the villagers marched to the rich man's summer home, which they first looted and then burned to the ground.

Luckily for the villagers, the rich man was not in residence at his summer home. Had he been, he would have been killed and could not have continued supporting them, as he did for many years thereafter.

## The Mislaid Mission

Three sergeants had been separated from their unit for several days, and had been wandering in the wilderness all that time with only meager rations.

"How can we get back in touch with our unit?" one of them asked through parched lips.

"Well," speculated another one of the sergeants, "if we could only remember what our orders read—you know, when they were tacked up on the bulletin board the day before we left. If we could remember them, we'd know what our mission was, and we could head in the direction of the objective, but I just can't remember."

"Neither can we," the other two sighed.

One of the sergeants slapped irritably at a fly which had been bothering him for some time. "I'll bet I remember what our mission was!" he shouted, a ferocious gleam kindling in his eyes. "Wasn't it to exterminate all these blasted flies? Yes! That's what it was!"

With that he fashioned a flyswatter out of his mess kit and began to run about furiously, swatting at every fly he could see—and at some he couldn't.

"No! No! No! That's not it! Come back and sit down," they shouted to him, but to no avail. He soon disappeared over the horizon, swatting flies.

"Well," said one of the two remaining sergeants, lying back in the sparse shade of a bush, "frankly, I don't care much about what our mission was, or about getting back to our unit. I kind of like it here with no general or second looeys to tell us what to do, so I'm just going to take advantage of that fact and get myself a little peace and quiet."

So saying, he went to sleep, leaving the third sergeant to ponder alone.

After several hours of fruitless pondering about their mislaid mission, the wakeful sergeant suddenly heard noises of troop movements in the distance. Excitedly he shook the second sergeant.

"Wake up! Wake up!" he shouted in his ear. "I've remembered what our mission is!"

"What is it?" the sleepy sergeant asked, rubbing his eyes and yawning.

"It's to defend! To *defend!*" he shouted triumphantly.

"To defend what? Where? Against what or whom?" the sleepy sergeant asked, not much impressed.

"What does all that folderol matter?" the active sergeant shouted with impatience. "Look! See on the horizon? The enemy advances upon us even now! Defend! Fire!"

The active sergeant took up his Browning automatic rifle and began to fire upon the advancing troops in rapid, deadly bursts. Truly he was a paragon of action, running first to the extreme right and firing from there, then running to the extreme left and firing from there. Finally, he hurried to the extreme center and fired there, with telling effect, from the hip.

"Stop! Stop! Cease fire!" shouted the sleepy sergeant, now sleepy no more. "I don't remember any orders like that. You may be making a mistake!"

But the active sergeant was so engrossed in what he had been doing that he could not hear his comrade speaking to him. He stopped only when all the troops were dead and lay in grotesque patterns upon the sand. Both sergeants ran up to look at the dead soldiers.

As they rolled one dead man over, they both gasped in horror.

"Gad, Sam," whispered the once-sleeping sergeant, "you've killed *our* boys!"

# Lying Offshore

A ship rocked slowly upon the greasy seas. Its sails were tattered, its masts spliced, and its hull leaky with worm-eaten planks, but still it stayed afloat. It had been sailing for many years—for generations, actually. Many years ago it had been loaded with food and medicine, and dispatched to find and to help the people of a lost colony. As it traveled far and wide, all its original crew except one had died, their places being taken by their children.

In the prow an old man, the last of the original crew, sat upon a coil of rope, his eyes struggling to pierce the fog.

Below decks, men, women, and children sat down to eat. Although the fare was meager, it was adequate, and all their faces shone with health.

The meal was almost over when both doors of the messroom were thrown open with a loud noise and a rush of wind. In the opening stood the old man, strange and wild, stronger than they had ever seen him, shouting, "We're *here!* We've arrived at land!"

"Land?" they asked, not moving from the table. "What land?"

"Why the land that we were sent to when this voyage began. And the lost colony is there waiting. I can hear them shouting from the shore!" shouted the old man, stamping his feet with impatience. "Quick! Let's make for the shore and unload the food and the medicine!"

The old man turned to run back up the gangway, but he stopped halfway up when he realized there had been no movement in the messroom. Slowly he returned to stare at them with wide, incredulous eyes, his mouth agape. "Didn't you hear me? Are you all deaf? I said we're here! The people we were sent out to help are only a few hundred yards away. But we must hurry, for they are all hungry and sick."

"I'm sure we'd all like to help these people," said one of the men, "but—as you can see—there's hardly enough food and medicine here to take care of us and our children."

"Besides," said one of the women, "we don't know what kind of people they are. Who knows *what* might happen if we landed and went among them?"

The old man staggered back as if he had been struck across the face. "But . . . but . . . it was for *them* that this voyage began in the first place so many years ago, for *them* that the ship was built, for *them* that the food and medicine were stowed aboard!"

"Yes, old man, I've heard *many* tales of our launching from my father and from the older men who are now dead," replied one of the younger men, "but there were so many different accounts that how can we be sure which one is right? Why risk our stores and provisions, perhaps even our lives, on something we may not even be supposed to do?"

"He's right! He's right!" shouted many of the others, now quite excitedly involved in the conversation.

"But look," said the old man, trying very hard to contain himself, "it's all very simple! As far as there not being enough food for us *and* them, much of what we have left is meant for *seed*. If we go ashore and *plant* it, then there will be more than enough for all of us. And on the matter of *why* the ship was launched in the first place—you have merely to look in the logbook. It's all there."

The old man, hoping he had settled the question, looked anxiously from face to face around the tables. There was a long, thoughtful silence.

Finally, a man who had gravitated to a position of leadership among them stood up, picking his teeth and frowning thoughtfully.

"Perhaps the old man is right," he said, loosening a juicy morsel from between two teeth. "At any rate, his suggestion merits investigation. What I propose is this: let us select from among ourselves a representative committee which will see if they can find the logbook, and then go into a thorough study of it, to see if they can determine whether we should land or not."

"A sensible idea!" they all cried, except the old man. "Let's do it!"

The old man, now frantic with hearing the cries from the shore, shouted, "What *is* this? What are you *doing?* Oh!" he said, backing away from them with horror in his eyes, "I can see that you don't really expect to do anything at all!" His back against a bulkhead, he clutched at his chest and slid weakly to the floor.

"Let me warn you then," he gasped. "The food will not last. It was meant to stay preserved only for the time it would take to get here. Now the food will begin to molder, and the medicines will separate and lose their strength. If you don't take the provisions ashore and share them now, they will soon no longer feed or cure even you!" With this, he died.

As the days and weeks passed, the ship continued to lie offshore. The committee continued to search the logbook, which they had soon found, hoping to come up with a report "in the near future." A few of the younger men and women, maddened with the waiting and lured irresistibly by the cries of hunger and pain from the shore, slipped away one night in the jolly boat with a few provisions, and were listed sorrowfully next day as "lost at sea."

True to the old man's dying prophecy, the food on board began to grow all manner of weird and exotic fungi, and the extensive stores of medicine seemed less and less able to cure the ills of the people. Also, the cries from the shore began to grow so much louder that even the deafest on board had to stuff his ears with cotton in order to sleep.

But no one seemed to be able to decide what to do.

# The Image Behind the Image

In the village of Tecoatl, the Conquistadores tore down the temple of Tlaloc atop the tallest pyramid and erected in its stead the small but magnificent Chapel of the Holy Virgin. When Father Anselmo finally arrived in the strange, steaming jungles, he found a touch of home in the familiar surroundings of the altar, nave, chancel, and in the beautiful image of the Holy Virgin affixed to the wall behind the altar. He was well pleased to celebrate the Mass in the little chapel day by day before the small group of faithful soldiers, some of whom were always present.

But when the garrison was off on a combat mission far to the south, Father Anselmo soon grew tired of celebrating the Mass in an empty chapel, so he went among the natives to invite them to come and worship with him. He found them a recalcitrant lot, however, who preferred to continue worshipping Tlaloc, even though his image had been smashed by the soldiers. Father Anselmo explained that the Holy Virgin would make their crops grow even better than had Tlaloc, since she was real and Tlaloc was only an image fashioned by men's minds and hands. But still the natives refused to enter the chapel.

Seeing the priest's untiring efforts to fill his chapel, the old *cacique* (or headman) of the village said to him one day, "I know how you can fill your temple to overflowing with my people."

"How?" asked the priest eagerly.

"I have noticed, in my secret visits to your place of worship, that the image of your Holy One is flat on the back where it touches the wall. In my house I have a fine image of Tlaloc, which is also flat on the back. If you would pull your image out from the wall just a bit, and if we were to put the image of Tlaloc there—the images back to back—then my people would come."

"But that would be unfitting!" protested Father Anselmo.

"Why," asked the old *cacique,* "when your image will entirely hide the smaller image of Tlaloc from view, and only my people will know it is there at all? To outward appearances nothing will have changed, except that your empty chapel will be full of reverent worshipers."

Moved by the vision of the chapel full of reverent worshipers, Father Anselmo consented.

Now, with a full chapel every time he celebrated the Mass, Father Anselmo was happy. The old *cacique* was happy. And the throng of natives, flocking to the chapel daily with their offerings of maize, fruit, and chickens, were happy too.

In fact, it would take a strange and cynical man indeed not to be happy over such a pleasant situation as that!

# The Sacred Priest
## and the Profane Hermit

In a certain city there was a priest who awoke on a morning plagued with a sense of undone duty toward one of his inactive parishioners, who had recently taken up the life of a hermit in a cave inside the city limits. The priest had put off confronting the hermit with the error of his ways, because the hermit was much older than he, and perhaps even wiser. But the priest decided to wait no longer, so he went up to the cave and entered it with a rush of words, because he was nervous.

"Do you not know that you cannot live the Christian life apart from the fellowship of other devout Christians? How do you hope to be saved if you remain aloof from the society of men, into which even God took up flesh and wandered? By all the saints, man, you are more aloof than God himself!"

The hermit meditated upon the priest's words for a while, as was his practice, and then he asked, "How do you spend your days, friend priest?"

"Why, doing the work of the church, of course," the priest answered, glad he had been asked. "All my evenings are occupied with important church meetings; my afternoons I spend in visiting church members, either at their homes or in the hospitals; and my mornings, from six until twelve," he went on, preening himself humbly, "are spent in my study poring over my Bible, the works of the church Fathers, books of current theological issues, missions, ethics, preaching, church history, and sermon illustrations. It makes for some very full and stimulating mornings. And you, brother hermit, what do you read? I see stacks of books against yonder wall."

"Oh," the hermit replied, with a deprecating gesture, "I read some of what you read, but not a bit so thoroughly or systematically I'm afraid. I spend quite a bit of my time on paperbacks and magazines, too."

"Paperbacks?" the priest gasped. "Oh, I see," he added, regaining his composure, "you mean those inexpensive editions of good, sound theological works from England?"

"No, not at all," the hermit answered. "They are mostly current plays, poetry, novels, and short stories."

"By all the saints, man," the priest spat, drawing himself up, "I had thought better of you than this! I had taken for granted that when you separated yourself from Christian society, at least you had done so to give yourself to serious contemplation! But you tell me now that you fritter away your time with frivolities—inanities!"

The hermit, who had thought he was only conversing, became aware from the attitude of the priest that he was really confessing. Therefore, not wishing his confession to be incomplete, he took a deep breath and added soberly, "And as for the magazines, I have my own subscriptions to *Esquire* and *Playboy*."

At this, the priest's eyes rolled back into his head and he neglected to breathe. He rocked upon his feet, and veins stood out upon his neck and forehead. He looked wildly about him (thinking that perchance he would see some of those foldout photographs hanging on the cave's walls—but to no avail). Then he backed jerkily out of the cave, brushing off the sleeves of his cassock with a look of horror and disgust upon his face.

"I had thought this the cave of a devout hermit," he shouted from outside the cave's entrance, "but now it's revealed to me for what it is—a literal den of iniquity! It's full not only of wicked worldliness, but also of downright pornography!"

These harsh words from a man of God cast the hermit into a sudden pit of doubt and self-accusation.

"Perhaps what you are saying is true, friend priest," the hermit said with bowed head. "Surely, I must have done wrong. You see, I got the impression from your own preaching (which some said was avant-garde and radical) that it is the calling of Christian men to serve the poor world and the worldlings in any good way that they could. So I decided to live apart, and spend my life in prayer for the world and for all men. 'But,' I asked myself, 'how are you to know what their troubles and sorrows are, and how to pray for their needs, if you spend all your time filling your mind only with the literature of the church? Would you not find out about men's problems and how to pray for their needs better if you *also* studied their own soul-outpourings?' I thus decided to immerse myself in what you, friend priest, have called their frivolities, inanities, and pornography."

The hermit looked up, tears brimming in his eyes. "But now," he said, "because of your words of brotherly concern, I doubt my decision. Perhaps it would be best for me to confine my reading to what you read."

The priest, mollified, allowed his frown to smooth, and said quite as smoothly, "I'm sorry that I spoke harshly, brother hermit. But it is sometimes necessary to do so in order to correct a brother's error."

The hermit burst into tears at the priest's kindness. When he had controlled himself, he said through broken sobbing, "Only one thing still bothers me."

"Yes?" smiled the priest, bending forward in eagerness to give the answer.

"Is it not possible that, if I no longer listen to what the world is crying about itself and listen only to what the church is saying to the world, I might become even more aloof than you say I am now from the society of men, into which (as you graciously reminded me) God himself took up flesh and wandered?"

Without another word, except a snort of disgust, the priest turned angrily and strode down the hill, his cassock flapping in the wind like the wings of a black eagle. As he went down to his house, he felt that even though he had apparently failed to convert the hermit, at least he was justified by his sincere attempt.

Meanwhile, back at the cave, the hermit was taking ashes from his fireplace and showering them upon his head, beating his breast in confusion and crying continuously, "Lord, be merciful unto me, a sinner!"

# Introduction to the Biblical Parables

In several of his parables, Jesus seems concerned about making his hearers think about his Word of Life and how it is intended to function among us—about the people of God and how they should live. These are *his* parables about *our* mission.

# *The Sower*

Again Jesus began to teach beside Lake Galilee. The crowd that gathered around him was so large that he got into a boat and sat in it. The boat was out in the water, and the crowd stood on the shore at the water's edge. He used parables to teach them many things, saying to them:

"Listen! Once there was a man who went out to sow grain. As he scattered the seed in the field, some of it fell along the path, and the birds came and ate it up. Some of it fell on rocky ground, where there was little soil. The seeds soon sprouted, because the soil wasn't deep. Then, when the sun came up, it burned the young plants; and because the roots had not grown deep enough, the plants soon dried up. Some of the seed fell among thorn bushes, which grew up and choked the plants, and they didn't bear grain. But some seeds fell in good soil, and the plants sprouted, grew, and bore grain: some had thirty grains, others sixty, and others one hundred."

And Jesus concluded, "Listen, then, if you have ears!"

MARK 4:1-9

27

# The Wicked Tenants

"Listen to another parable," Jesus said. "There was once a landowner who planted a vineyard, put a fence around it, dug a hole for the wine press, and built a watchtower. Then he rented the vineyard to tenants and left home on a trip. When the time came to gather the grapes, he sent his slaves to the tenants to receive his share of the harvest. The tenants grabbed his slaves, beat one, killed another, and stoned another. Again the man sent other slaves, more than the first time, and the tenants treated them the same way. Last of all he sent his son to them. 'Surely they will respect my son,' he said. But when the tenants saw the son, they said to themselves, 'This is the owner's son. Come on, let's kill him, and we will get his property!' So they grabbed him, threw him out of the vineyard, and killed him.

"Now, when the owner of the vineyard comes, what will he do to those tenants?" Jesus asked.

"He will certainly kill those evil men," they answered, "and rent the vineyard out to other tenants, who will give him his share of the harvest at the right time."

Jesus said to them, "Haven't you ever read what the Scriptures say?
'The stone which the builders rejected as worthless
    turned out to be the most important of all.
This was done by the Lord;
    what a wonderful sight it is!'

"And so I tell you," added Jesus, "the Kingdom of God will be taken away from you and given to a people who will produce the proper fruits."

The chief priests and the Pharisees heard Jesus' parables and knew that he was talking about them, so they tried to arrest him. But they were afraid of the crowds, who considered Jesus to be a prophet.
MATT. 21:33-46

# The Great Supper

Then Jesus said to his host, ". . . When you give a feast, invite the poor, the crippled, the lame, and the blind; and you will be blessed, because they are not able to pay you back. God will repay you on the day the good people rise from death."

When one of the men sitting at the table heard this, he said to Jesus, "How happy are those who will sit down at the feast in the Kingdom of God!"

Jesus said to him, "There was once a man who was giving a great feast to which he invited many people. When it was time for the feast, he sent his servant to tell his guests, 'Come, everything is ready!' But they all began, one after another, to make excuses. The first one told the servant, 'I have bought a field and must go and look at it; please accept my apologies.' Another one said, 'I have bought five pairs of oxen and am on my way to try them out; please accept my apologies.' Another one said, 'I have just gotten married, and for that reason I cannot come.' The servant went back and told all this to his master. The master was furious and said to his servant, 'Hurry out to the streets and alleys of the town, and bring back the poor, the crippled, the blind, and the lame.' Soon the servant said, 'Your order has been carried out, sir, but there is room for more.' So the master said to the servant, 'Go out to the country roads and lanes and make people come in, so that my house will be full. I tell you all that none of those men who were invited will taste my dinner!'"

LUKE 14:12–24

# The Good Samaritan

But the teacher of the Law wanted to justify himself, so he asked Jesus, "Who is my neighbor?"

Jesus answered, "There was once a man who was going down from Jerusalem to Jericho when robbers attacked him, stripped him, and beat him up, leaving him half dead. It so happened that a priest was going down that road; but when he saw the man, he walked on by on the other side. In the same way a Levite also came there, went over and looked at the man, and then walked on by on the other side. But a Samaritan who was traveling that way came upon the man, and when he saw him, his heart was filled with pity. He went over to him, poured oil and wine on his wounds and bandaged them; then he put the man on his own animal and took him to an inn, where he took care of him. The next day he took out two silver coins and gave them to the innkeeper. 'Take care of him,' he told the innkeeper, 'and when I come back this way, I will pay you whatever else you spend on him.'"

And Jesus concluded, "In your opinion, which one of these three acted like a neighbor toward the man attacked by the robbers?"

The teacher of the Law answered, "The one who was kind to him."

Jesus replied, "You go, then, and do the same."

LUKE 10:29-37

## The Pharisee and the Tax Collector

Jesus also told this parable to people who were sure of their own goodness and despised everybody else. "Once there were two men who went up to the Temple to pray: one was a Pharisee, the other a tax collector. The Pharisee stood apart by himself and prayed, 'I thank you, God, that I am not greedy, dishonest, or an adulterer, like everybody else. I thank you that I am not like that tax collector over there. I fast two days a week, and I give you one tenth of all my income.' But the tax collector stood at a distance and would not even raise his face to heaven, but beat on his breast and said, 'God, have pity on me, a sinner!' I tell you," said Jesus, "the tax collector, and not the Pharisee, was in the right with God when he went home. For everyone who makes himself great will be humbled, and everyone who humbles himself will be made great."

LUKE 18:9-14

**THEME TWO**

# Love Versus Bargaining

# Introduction to the Modern Parables

We use the word *love* in so many different ways that it is hard to find a good definition for the word. But we all know what it's like to *feel* loved or unloved. We feel loved when we know that we are cherished *for ourselves* and not for what we can do for the other. If someone gives of themselves only for what they expect others to give in return, that's not love—that's just trading. Is much of our so-called "loving" of God just an attempt to get something for ourselves? It is said that John Calvin, the great religious leader, asked his young preachers one final question before they graduated from his schooling to go out into the world: "If you knew it would be for the glory of God, would you be willing to be damned to hell for eternity?" That question really must have separated the loving sheep from all the bargaining goats.

# *A Bargain with God*

Simon Pure dropped in to Penny Poor's store one day. He clucked his tongue at the dust on Penny's showcases, and shook his head and sighed at the many bare shelves.

"Why do you suppose it is," he asked poor old Penny, "that your store isn't as prosperous as mine? We both started out at about the same time, and with the same capital—almost nothing. But now I have a lovely store that nets me forty thousand a year after taxes, and you have only this dusty, half-stocked hole which does well to pay your rent for you. Why is that, Penny?"

Penny stared vacantly and shrugged his thin shoulders.

"I've often wondered that myself, Simon, but I don't know. Perhaps if I did know the answer, I could do something about it."

Simon studied his gold wristwatch with the diamond numbers on it for a second, and then he leaned close to Penny's ear, whispering a gust of mouthwash odor which carried on it these words, "I'll tell you the secret."

Penny's widening eyes swiveled to Simon's face. "Please do," he implored.

Simon sat down on the edge of the counter, pulling the creases of his trousers up smartly.

"There's one difference between the way *you* went into business and the way *I* went into business, Penny," he said, smiling benignly at the poor little fellow. "When I started *my* store twenty-three years ago, I took God as my partner."

Penny didn't know whether Simon was joking or not, but when Simon just let those words hang in the dusty air, and neither laughed nor qualified them, Penny swallowed and said, "Well, how did you do that?"

"Easy," said Simon, "if you know the Bible. There's where the secret is. Twenty-three years ago I promised God that if he'd prosper me in my business, I'd give him a tenth of the profits and spend a month every summer doing missionary work for him."

"So *that's* where you go every summer," murmured Penny.

"Yes," beamed Simon, "and we've both kept our ends of the bargain all these years. Well," looking again at his watch, "I've got to be going now. But you know the secret now, too, so I'm expecting to see some changes around here next time I come to see you." Laughing warmly, Simon left Penny to ponder his words.

Penny did ponder. He thought of how he had supported his little inner-city church for those twenty-three years, sometimes borrowing off his insurance policy in order to pay some bills that the dwindling congregation couldn't seem to pay. Penny supposed that he had spent more than a tenth of his time working to keep that little church going. Plus that, he had always looked upon his store-keeping as a sort of a ministry too—keeping people from buying things they didn't need or couldn't afford, extending interest-free credit to people who seemed to need it, and being a kind of resident marriage counselor to the young husbands and wives in the neighborhood. Penny thought about God and God's abilities, and he was mildly surprised that it had never occurred to him to question God's beneficence. But when he did think of it, Penny just couldn't bring himself to blame God for the dust on his showcases or the empty spaces on his shelves. The thought of himself praying to God to prosper his business crossed Penny's mind unbidden. It embarrassed Penny, then caused him to shake with laughter at his silly old self.

Three months later Simon Pure's store burned to the ground, and the skimpy insurance policies on it didn't pay off half the value lost.

Penny tried to visit Simon to cheer him up, but after knocking at Simon's door on three occasions and getting no answer, he finally sent him a letter of condolences. Penny wrote some things about God, and beginning again, and about how he would be glad to help Simon start a new store—such things as that.

He received a one-line letter from Simon by return mail. It said, "There is no God!"

# The Just Merchant

There was a certain merchant who lived in a land in which all people were equal, but "some were more equal than others."

In an attempt to adjust the embarrassing imbalance in equality, the government of that land declared that no businesses or industries should practice discrimination in their hiring policies. "In the future," the government directive stated, "all jobs shall be filled without regard to the applicant's ethnic origins, religious creed, or sex."

Although the merchant greeted this decree with some enthusiasm (since he truly wanted everyone to be equally equal), many of his peers were not so enthusiastic.

"Why, it's unfair, heavy-handed, and I don't know what else," said another merchant, "for the government to tell private business whom to hire and whom not to!"

"Yeah," agreed a manufacturer, "we all want to see equal opportunities given to all. Of course we do. But this is something which we should work out among *ourselves* without the government imposing it upon us from above!"

"Yes," shouted another man, a wholesaler, "we all know that you can't legislate morals anyway, and this is basically a moral issue!"

After listening to the statements of his peers, the merchant thoughtfully stroked his beard and said, "Perhaps you're right. Perhaps this is something we should be doing among ourselves, rather than having to be legislated into it."

So saying, the merchant returned to his store and, after seeing to it that all his employment practices should thenceforward be carried out on a nondiscriminatory basis, he sent out letters to all the manu-

36

facturers and wholesalers who supplied him with merchandise. The letters stated that his new policy would be not to buy from any wholesalers or manufacturers who practiced any kind of discrimination in their hiring.

After having done what he could to bring about justice in this manner "on a local level and without requiring government enforcement," the manufacturer was somewhat surprised when some of his peers greeted him, not with congratulations, but with rage and scorn.

"That's not a matter which private business should tamper with!" said one.

"Bad taste!" said another.

"You're trying to do something which only the government has the right or the necessity to do!" said yet another.

# *Jake and Easy*

A certain man had two sons.

As the man was getting old and tired, he called his sons to him one day. Jake came into his father's office nattily attired in a Brooks Bros. suit, silk tie, and shiny black shoes. Easy, the other brother, slouched into the office—a mass of bells, bangles, hair, and beads— barefooted.

"My boys," said the father, "I've been running this business for forty-five years in this little neighborhood, but now I'm too old, and you boys are just the right ages to take over the business. What do you say?"

"Sure, Daddy," said Jake with a smile that can best be described as oily.

"Forget it, man," drawled Easy. "I'm not *about* to cop out and become a money-grubber!"

"But, Easy," his father pleaded, "these people need help! Other stores in this area bleed them—you should pardon the expression— white by demanding exorbitant interest rates and repossessing merci- lessly the moment a payment is just one day late. They know that this store will treat them fairly, as human beings. This business doesn't just take selling ability, it takes *heart!*"

"I got heart, man," said Easy, "and that's why I say 'Cool it.' "

With a weary sigh, the old man handed the keys over to Jake.

"I've got heart, Daddy," cooed Jake.

"Such a heart," the old man shouted back over his shoulder as he went out the alley door, "a marble *statue* should have!"

38

Jake bought out Easy's share of the business, and instituted some new policies at the old furniture store. He would buy a plywood and pine dining room suite from the manufacturer for $47.50, and sell it to a customer for $147.50—$5 down and $5 per week for 36 weeks. If hard times set in and the customer was unable to pay, Jake gave ten days' notice and then repossessed the furniture. Sometimes he could sell one suite of dining room furniture as many as seven times before it fell apart. Jake was really making the old business prosper.

Meanwhile Easy had used the money from his share of the business to buy a big old house in the neighborhood. He let poor people flop there for nothing, and always had this huge pot of spaghetti boiling on the stove. When neighbors had trouble with their landlords, Easy went with them to city hall. When some of his neighbors saved their money and got rich enough to move out of the neighborhood, Easy "fronted" for them so they could get a new house wherever they wanted. And during the July riots, it was Easy who dragged Jake's "accounts payable" files out into the alley and set fire to them.

Now, which son do you think pleased his father the most?

# The Children

An old man, ripe in years, called his four children to his bedside. "The doctors," he told them weakly, "say that I have only a few days to live, and I wanted to take a good look at all of you once more."

Upon hearing these words, each of the old man's children was filled with emotion. For the youngest son, Edward, the emotion was grief. But for the older two sisters and brother, the emotion was largely greed, for the father was very rich.

"Here, Daddy," said one sister, "let me fluff up your pillow."

"Daddy dear, wouldn't you like me to fix you some nice broth?" asked the other sister.

"Is there something I could do around the house or the office for you, Dad?" asked the older brother. "We all want to help, you know."

This attitude on the part of the three older children was rather confusing to the old man, since none of them had bothered to visit him or even write to him for the past several years.

"Yes, Daddy, we all want to help you, except . . ." snipped the brother, pointing his nose accusingly at Edward, who was still sitting and staring sorrowfully at his father. Unable to bear what he saw was happening, Edward kissed his father and left the house.

"Tell him to come back," whispered the father.

"Why do you need *him?*" asked the older brother. "He's never been of any help to you, has he? Besides, you have us with you now."

The two sisters and the one brother did not leave their father's bedside for the next three days and nights, fussing over him continually. Edward came to pay brief, nervous visits to his father twice. On one visit the father said, "Take care of the family, Edward."

"I will, Father," Edward promised.

"Huh! He can hardly take care of himself," snorted the older brother.

On Edward's other visit his father said, "Take care of the business, Edward."

"I will, Father," Edward promised.

"The business! Fat chance!" rasped one of the sisters. "He's never even earned a penny in his life!"

On the third day of the father's illness the older sister asked him—for the fiftieth time in three days—if he had thought about his will. Usually the father had pretended not to hear the question. But now, sensing that he had not long to live, the father called for pen and paper. Feebly, he wrote. Then, with a sigh, he fell back upon his pillows.

"Uh, did you make it out?" asked the younger sister.

"Mm, yes. Aren't you going to tell us?" asked the other sister.

Expectantly, their faces wreathed with wan smiles, they gathered around the bed as their father unfolded the piece of paper.

"I have left everything to Edward," he read weakly.

"Edward!" they all shouted.

While one sister fell into a fit of weeping, the other sister and the brother began arguing with the old man, protesting against his judgment, reminding him of their loving service and of Edward's long absences and general uselessness.

Finally the old man shushed them long enough to say, "Never, in all your lives, have you loved me. You have only loved what I could do for you. Edward, however, has cared little or nothing for what I could do for him. He has loved me for myself. You have your own inheritance, one you have made for yourselves—an inheritance of greed, envy, bitterness, and emptiness."

After Edward came into his inheritance, they all refused his offers of help and had nothing but evil things to say of him.

## The Two Magistrates

Two magistrates were visiting together on the third floor of the municipal building.

"I had an interesting case this morning," said one magistrate, cutting the tip from a cigar, then lighting the cigar carefully. "A young woman—poor, ragged, very little education, no job ability except for the most menial tasks. She had gotten into some small troubles, as much because of her poverty and helplessness as anything, and (puff) I had to decide (puff, puff) what to do with her."

"And what *did* you do with her?" asked the other magistrate, looking out the window at the teeming sidewalks below.

"Well, she was guilty as charged so I sentenced her and then suspended the sentence. Calling her into my chambers, I gave her some good, sound advice about staying out of trouble, holding up her head, self-respect, and all that," he puffed, musing through clouds of smoke. "And then I saw to it that she'd have a regular monthly income on which she can live modestly, but respectably."

"How did you do that?" inquired the other. "Did you find her a job?"

"No. As I said, she's only fit for the most menial tasks, and I had decided that her basic problem was one of self-respect, which certainly wasn't going to be helped by putting her back in some ignominious job. So I was able to secure her a monthly income through a private charity organization with which I have some connections."

The other magistrate did not comment. After a silence that became uncomfortable, the first magistrate said, "Well, I guess you would have decided differently, huh?"

"I'm not sure what I would have done," said the other magistrate. "It's a difficult problem, but I doubt that I would have decided as you did. I don't know but that you may have pushed her even further into her problems, rather than relieving her of them."

"Why, what do you mean?" asked the cigar-smoking magistrate. "I did the best I could for the poor woman. I felt some sense of responsibility for her, so I wasn't going to throw her back into the same situation, or just wash my hands of her! You can't just turn your back on the needs of the poor!"

"I know, I know," said the other magistrate, attempting to calm his now agitated friend. "It was *good* for you to feel responsible for her, and to try to do something to alleviate her condition. But it seems to me the question is not just, 'Am I responsible for this person or not?' but that it also is a question of, 'What is the *best way* for me to act responsibly toward this person?' If you were really concerned about her self-regard, you might better have found her a way to train herself for some skilled work, rather than merely giving her an assured monthly income."

"Oh, I thought of that," said the first magistrate, frowning at the end of his cigar. "But you know how those people are. She would have dropped out of a training program within a week, and then gotten right back into her old troubles. Besides," he chuckled, "she didn't seem at all disappointed to receive the money, and she hasn't yet tried to give any of it back!"

The conversation ended. The two magistrates left the office, entered the elevator, and went each to his own home.

## Introduction to the Biblical Parables

The strongest, clearest concept of God which Jesus gave us was of God as the loving father of us all. In several of Jesus' parables, this concept of God as father is used to show what children of such a loving father should *be* and *do.*

## *The Laborers in the Vineyard*

"The Kingdom of heaven is like this. Once there was a man who went out early in the morning to hire some men to work in his vineyard. He agreed to pay them the regular wage, a silver coin a day, and sent them to work in his vineyard. He went out again to the marketplace at nine o'clock and saw some men standing there doing nothing, so he told them, 'You also go and work in the vineyard, and I will pay you a fair wage.' So they went. Then at twelve o'clock and again at three o'clock he did the same thing. It was nearly five o'clock when he went to the marketplace and saw some other men still standing there. 'Why are you wasting the whole day here doing nothing?' he asked them. 'No one hired us,' they answered. 'Well, then, you go and work in the vineyard,' he told them.

"When evening came, the owner told his foreman, 'Call the workers and pay them their wages, starting with those who were hired last and ending with those who were hired first.' The men who had begun to work at five o'clock were paid a silver coin each. So when the men who were the first to be hired came to be paid, they thought they would get more; but they too were given a silver coin each. They took their

money and started grumbling against the employer. 'These men who were hired last worked only one hour,' they said, 'while we put up with a whole day's work in the hot sun—yet you paid them the same as you paid us!' 'Listen, friend,' the owner answered one of them, 'I have not cheated you. After all, you agreed to do a day's work for one silver coin. Now take your pay and go home. I want to give this man who was hired last as much as I gave you. Don't I have the right to do as I wish with my own money? Or are you jealous because I am generous?' "

And Jesus concluded, "So those who are last will be first, and those who are first will be last."

MATT. 20:1–16

## The Two Sons

"Now, what do you think? There was once a man who had two sons. He went to the older one and said, 'Son, go and work in the vineyard today.' 'I don't want to,' he answered, but later he changed his mind and went. Then the father went to the other son and said the same thing. 'Yes, sir,' he answered, but he did not go. Which one of the two did what his father wanted?"

"The older one," they answered.

So Jesus said to them, "I tell you: the tax collectors and the prostitutes are going into the Kingdom of God ahead of you. For John the Baptist came to you showing you the right path to take, and you would not believe him; but the tax collectors and the prostitutes believed him. Even when you saw this, you did not later change your minds and believe him."

MATT. 21:28–32

## The Prodigal Son

Jesus went on to say, "There was once a man who had two sons. The younger one said to him, 'Father, give me my share of the property now.' So the man divided his property between his two sons. After a few days the younger son sold his part of the property and left home with the money. He went to a country far away, where he wasted his money in reckless living. He spent everything he had. Then a severe famine spread over that country, and he was left without a thing. So he went to work for one of the citizens of that country, who sent him out to his farm to take care of the pigs. He wished he could fill himself with the bean pods the pigs ate, but no one gave him anything to eat. At last he came to his senses and said, 'All my father's hired workers have more than they can eat, and here I am about to starve! I will get up and go to my father and say, "Father, I have sinned against God and against you. I am no longer fit to be called your son; treat me as one of your hired workers."' So he got up and started back to his father.

"He was still a long way from home when his father saw him; his heart was filled with pity, and he ran, threw his arms around his son, and kissed him. 'Father,' the son said, 'I have sinned against God and against you. I am no longer fit to be called your son.' But the father called to his servants. 'Hurry!' he said. 'Bring the best robe and put it on him. Put a ring on his finger and shoes on his feet. Then go and get the prize calf and kill it, and let us celebrate with a feast! For this son of mine was dead, but now he is alive; he was lost, but now he has been found.' And so the feasting began.

"In the meantime the older son was out in the field. On his way back, when he came close to the house, he heard the music and dancing. So he called one of the servants and asked him, 'What's going on?' 'Your brother has come back home,' the servant answered, 'and your father has killed the prize calf, because he got him back safe and sound.' The older brother was so angry that he would not go into the house; so his father came out and begged him to come in. But he spoke back to his father, 'Look, all these years I have worked for you like a slave, and I have never disobeyed your orders. What have you given me? Not even a goat for me to have a feast with my friends! But this son of yours wasted all your property on prostitutes, and when he comes back home, you kill the prize calf for him!' 'My son,' the father answered, 'you are always here with me, and everything I have is yours. But we had to celebrate and be happy, because your brother was dead, but now he is alive; he was lost, but now he has been found.' "

LUKE 15:11–32

# Grace Versus the Law

# Introduction to the Modern Parables

"The Law" was the approximately 669 rules and regulations which the most devout Jews of the Old Testament lived by—all growing, more or less, from the original Ten Commandments. Jesus brought only two Great Commandments—having to do with loving God, one another, and ourselves—which were the actual fulfillment of all the old rules and regulations. But it is so much clearer, and often easier, to live by rules than it is to live by love that we often find ourselves broken into two different camps—those who live by the old way, mistrusting the new, and those who live by the new way, seeming to threaten the old.

# *The Innovator*

It had been a long, long time since such a crime had been committed; and, as punishment, the Innovator would receive a sentence which had not been heard of for a long, long time—not since the days of the great-great-greats. It was a sentence at once so terrible and horrifying in its aspect that the High Court and the C.D.'s felt that it justly fit the nauseous and perverse crime of innovation. The punishment was to be expulsion from the Dome!

The citizens lined both sides of the street, their expressions a mixture of hatred and awe as their eyes followed the progress of the Innovator, escorted by a cordon of C.D.'s, toward the Lox. Gamblers in the crowd were busily making book on how long it would take the Innovator to die once he was outside the Dome, and on whether it would be death from Fallout, Poisongas, or perhaps even from a Wildbeast. There was no doubt that he would soon die (for imbedded deep in the mind of each citizen was the truism that no human life could possibly exist outside the protection of the Dome—that beloved plastic canopy erected by their great-great-great-grandfathers, which stretched over the city from limit to limit, cuddling it in a benevolent, airtight grip). The only question was, How long would death take to come and in what form?

Some of the sadists in the crowd had scraped through the thick crust of dirt on the Dome wall near the Lox so that they could see the Outside, and were selling places at these peepholes for a nice sum.

The C.D.'s and their prisoner had arrived at the Lox. The crowd retreated now in a minor panic for fear that some poisonous fume might enter the Dome when the Lox was opened. The mechanism was still good, although it had been unused for all these generations. At a press of the button from the Chief, the thick transparent door of the Lox swung jerkily open. The Innovator, with a last mournful look over his shoulder, was pushed rather roughly into the small compartment. The door was then shut, and the citizens held their collective breath as the Chief touched the next button. The outer door swung open with a great hissing into that unhealthily green Outside.

At his first breath of the Outside's air, the Innovator fell headlong, coughing, doubled up with a giant convulsion. The C.D.'s nodded their heads, pleased, and there was a clamor almost like a cheer that arose from those at the peepholes as they watched him and their wrist-watches to determine the exact second of his last gasp.

But then the terrible thing happened. The Innovator slowly raised his head from the dust and, with the beginnings of a smile of great joy upon his face, filled his lungs deeply. His eyes grew wide. He sat up, and they could see his chest bulging with gulp after gulp of that alien air. The people were so startled that they cried aloud when he suddenly jumped from a sitting position straight up, coming down in the first steps of a wild dance.

"It must have hit his brain first," said one spectator, his nose flattened against the Dome wall.

The Innovator stopped his dance abruptly as he turned to see the faces peering out at him. He smiled at them—a broad, toothy smile with no malice in it at all. He even opened his arms wide to them, making a beckoning gesture!

At this point, many of those watching him could take it no more, and they turned away to go back to their homes, shuddering with a nausea of fear.

After making many gestures of well-being to those amazed and still uncomprehending faces, the Innovator snapped his fingers and stooped to pick up a stick. With it, he wrote in large letters upon the ground, "Come on out—the air is *fine!*"

One after another, shocked faces left the peepholes, not to return.

Again he wrote in the dirt, this time with more urgency, "It is *fresh* air—not poison."

Still more left.

This time, almost frantic to make himself understood, he wrote, "You don't *need* the Dome anymore. You can live Outside! It is *better* out here!"

With this, *every* face disappeared from the clear places in the grimy walls, and the Innovator was left alone in the Outside with its brilliant sun, its fresh and moving air, its trees and plants three times the size of those inside the Dome, and its birds and animals.

The newspapers the next morning carried grisly stories of the Innovator's immediate death outside the Lox. The city fathers decided in an emergency session that the interior of the Dome should be painted opaquely to a height of twenty feet all around. And those watchers who could not be scared into abject secrecy were interned in the asylum, where talk of living outside the Dome could be taken for what it was—the raving of a lunatic.

# The Educated Medicine Man

Mwambo was a medicine man for his people, the Itiku. Coming as he did from a long line of medicine men, Mwambo had quite a sense of vocation about his work. He saw that the spells, incantations, gestures, potions, and so forth, that his father and grandfather had taught him were really unable to cure most of the diseases and problems which his people brought to him day by day. So Mwambo spent seven years away from his people studying medicine at Johns Hopkins.

Actually, it had not bothered his patients at all that Mwambo was not able to heal them. It was so much a part of tribal tradition that sick people came to the Medicine Man, who recited ancient words and performed ancient actions, that when the people went away—still sick—no one seemed to want anything more from him than the small comfort they received from having him do what was expected. However, his inability to heal *did* bother Mwambo. This is why he decided to spend those years at Johns Hopkins learning the best ways to heal elephantiasis, leprosy, malaria, sleeping sickness, and other common diseases of his people.

You can imagine Mwambo's disappointment when he returned to his tribe, began to practice his new really-healing medicine—and was rejected for his trouble.

"Where are the rattling gourds and the masks your father and grandfather wore?" they asked petulantly.

"I come here needing *junukula* root powdered in monkey blood, and you stick me with a needle!" they protested.

"What we need around here is a new medicine man," they finally all agreed, "an old one who can shout and cry and carry on loudly with the spirits!"

"Yes," gummed an old man, "I *love* a good show!"

For a while Mwambo tried to mollify his people by shaking a gourd and muttering incantations while he gave them intravenous injections, but he soon became ashamed of himself and stopped.

When his people finally stopped coming to him altogether and refused to pay for his cures, Mwambo became a tanner of hides. His courses in chemistry at Johns Hopkins prepared him to do this excellently.

# The Diamond

A tattered prospector entered the Great Glass City one day. Riding his mule down streets between dazzling glass buildings, he shouted, "I've found it—the stone of great price!"

A few curious passers-by stopped and crowded around him.

"Look!" he shouted ecstatically, holding a large uncut diamond before their gaze. "It's a diamond!"

"Looks just like glass to me," said one lay expert, "and downright inferior glass, at that. All melted looking. Must have been fused by the Blast. Curious."

With this assessment, the crowd began to disperse.

"No! No! Look again!" cried the prospector. "It's valuable, exceedingly valuable!"

"If you want to see something exceedingly valuable, take a gander at *this!*" said a millionaire in the crowd, extending a knuckle circled by a large, ruby-colored, cut-glass ring.

After the "oooh's" and "aaah's" of the crowd died down, the prospector protested, "No! My diamond is far more valuable than your glass, no matter how beautiful your glass, nor how ugly my stone. Here, let me show you," he said, taking the millionaire's ring firmly in his grasp. With his diamond the prospector scratched a very small "x" on the surface of the ruby-colored glass.

"There! See?" he said, stepping back from his work. "Do you see *now* how the diamond is greater than the glass? Diamond scratches glass, but glass can't scratch diamond!"

"Ye gods, you stupid idiot!" screamed the millionaire, looking closely at his ring. "You've ruined a ten-thousand-dollar work of the glassmaker's art!"

The prospector was thrown into prison for three years.

At the end of the third year, when he was released from prison, the prospector marched straightaway to enact a plan he had been formulating all these years in the dungeon. Boldly he approached the Wondrous Shrine of Multicolored Glass at the center of the Great Glass City. (The residents had a habit of gathering there on their day off to watch the amazing display of colored lights on the colored glass, and then going home with a good feeling.) The prospector stepped resolutely up to the mammoth center panel of the glass shrine and with his diamond inscribed an eight-foot circle in its surface. Then he tapped the glass lightly with his forefinger. The sound of shattering glass brought a mob on the run. Pleased at the response, the prospector held the diamond aloft and was about to begin speaking to the people when they all cried out, as if with one voice, "Just *look* at what you've done to our shrine!"

With this they began pelting him with glass cobblestones, old bottles, and shards from the shattered shrine until he was quite covered by them, and quite dead. Only the diamond, still clutched in the prospector's dead fist, projected above the pile of vitreous debris.

In the days that followed the incident, some heathens, heretics, atheists, doubters, and malcontents in that great city began to form a society devoted to the carrying on of the prospector's message about diamond being more valuable than glass. They also devoted themselves to the living-out of the implications of such a revolutionary thesis. And so they too were persecuted, and many were killed. (It may be of passing interest to some readers to note that, rather than being called "diamond-lovers," they were called "glass-haters.")

But posterity has been more kind to the prospector and his memory. Around that original pile of glass, still topped with the bone-held diamond, is today a large and most impressive shrine of the finest multicolored glass that money can buy. The residents of the Great Glass City have a habit of gathering there on their day off to watch the spectacular displays of colored lights on the colored glass, and then going home with a good feeling.

# Creatures of Habit

Hiram was a good man—a good farmer too. The crops had paid off well at the last harvest, and he and his wife felt quite snug and secure in their little home now that the winter was coming on.

Only one thing bothered Hiram—the old barn. Its roof was leaky, there were a few boards rotted off the sides, and the dirt floor was uneven so that puddles collected when it rained and soon turned into indoor quagmires. Hiram was a sensitive soul, who really loved his animals, and he winced to remember last winter when the worst storm blew sleet right through the old barn from one end to the other. The horses' water froze solid, and the little calves had ugly yellow icicles hanging from their muzzles.

Rising from his chair so quickly that he startled his wife, Hiram went to the phone and called Moco Edwards.

"That new barn I was talking to you about?" he reminded Moco. "I want it. Start right away so's it'll be finished before real cold weather sets in."

Nothing had pleased Hiram quite so much in a long time as watching that new barn go up. It pleased Moco too, because Hiram had insisted that nothing but the best materials and workmanship go into it. He and his wife were going to be mighty comfortable this winter in their house, Hiram reasoned, so why shouldn't his animals be comfortable too? He even had a thermostatically controlled heater installed in the new barn.

As it happened, the finishing touches on the new barn were completed just the day before the first cold snap was due to hit. An orderly man who liked to do things one clear step at a time, Hiram had Moco's workmen tear down the old barn that very day, leaving nothing but the outline of the old foundation.

That night Hiram proudly ushered his animals into their new home and pulled the doors shut, warm and tight. In his warm bed Hiram enjoyed not having to worry about his animals, and not feeling guilty about them being in a cold, drafty barn while he was in a snug house.

Next morning Hiram and the Mrs. set out early for town, leaving the barn doors open for the animals in case it should turn bad. While they were in town the wind began to blow, it began to rain, and the temperature dropped to freezing, turning the rain into sleet. Hiram didn't feel a bit uneasy though, thinking of his cattle and horses filing into the new barn.

When they returned to the farm early that evening, Hiram went out to the barn. When his eyes grew accustomed to the darkness of the warm inside, he saw that there wasn't a single animal there.

Puzzled and frightened he ran outside to scan the fields, seeing nothing. Then, behind the barn he saw all his animals. Miserable, huddled together, with drifts of sleet and snow heaped upon their backs, his cattle and horses stood within the vague outline of the foundation where the old barn had once stood.

# Confession
## Is Good for the Cell

Hymie was dragged into the prison kicking and screaming.

"But I'm *innocent* I tell you!" he shouted for the seven hundred and fifty-fifth time as the turnkey slammed his cell door.

"Yeah, we're *all* innocent, buddy," came the harsh voice of Hymie's next-cell neighbor. "I been here on a bum rap for fifteen years now—as innocent as the warden though I am—maybe innocenter!"

After a few weeks of screaming himself hoarse about his innocence, Hymie finally settled down to a routine that divided equal time between brooding over the injustice of it all and making feverish plans for getting the truth of his innocence before the right people. He spent many hours daydreaming of the governor's embarrassment when he hand-delivered the pardon to Hymie's cell. The governor would sputter and fumble and blush in an agony of self-reproach over imprisoning such a noble, innocent man, while Hymie would keep a stern and unreadable face. The governor would offer all kinds of enticements to mollify Hymie—new cars, a fine suburban home with swimming pool and pool table, a setup into his own little business—but no, Hymie would sue. His revenge would be as monumental as the injustice they had wreaked upon him. Hymie's little eyes glittered in the gloom of his cell as he drank in the mental picture of the day when his innocence would triumph.

In the meantime, Hymie did what he could on the home front. When he wasn't writing ten-page letters to senators and congressmen, he was at his post at his cell door shouting his innocence to everyone who passed by. When he didn't receive replies from most of his letters, he accused the warden of tampering with the federal mails. He shouted that too.

One day when Hymie had been locked up in his cell for almost a year, his eyes became tired from following the long letter he was writing with a stubby pencil. To rest his eyes, he went to his cell window and looked out and down to the courtyard. The sight of grass greening and buds popping shocked him!

Somehow he had forgotten that there was an outside, or at least that life, time, and the world were still going on beyond his bars. Because his own life had been stopped in mid-beat by his imprisonment, he had let himself imagine that the whole world had stopped too—as if waiting with caught breath for that glorious day of the triumph of Hymie's innocence, that day when he would emerge from the hated prison.

It was too much for Hymie—the grass, the buds, everything living and growing and changing but him. He was trapped. It wasn't the world that hung in suspended animation while Hymie busily scribbled and shouted; it was Hymie who was trapped, immobile, like a bee in amber, while the rest of the world seethed by and around him. With a gasp Hymie swept the carefully lettered pages from his bunk and fell groaning into it.

It was dark in the cell by the time that supper came.

"Here you go, Mr. Innocent," the turnkey joked as he slid Hymie's tray through the slot in the iron door.

"I'm not innocent," Hymie croaked, weary with it all. "I'm guilty. Guilty as hell."

"What did you say?" the turnkey asked, strangely excited, holding his breath to catch the soft answer.

"Guilty," sighed Hymie. "I'm guilty."

Immediately there was a rattling of the key in the lock, and when Hymie raised his head the door didn't look right. When he got up and gave the door a tentative push, it swung open broadly into the dusky, deserted corridor.

Peeping timidly down the corridor, Hymie saw that other gates were hanging open before him all the way to the front gate. There was still enough sunlight left to give him a glimpse of the greening grass and the bursting buds beyond.

## Introduction to the Biblical Parables

In Jesus' day, the Scribes and Pharisees were the most religious and law-abiding people of the Jewish community. Jesus' agonizing effort to show them "a better way" is amply exhibited in the following parables, which are also meant to show us that "better way."

## Woes to the Pharisees

"How terrible for you, teachers of the Law and Pharisees! You hypocrites! You clean the outside of your cup and plate, while the inside is full of what you have gotten by violence and selfishness. Blind Pharisee! Clean what is inside the cup first, and then the outside will be clean too!

"How terrible for you, teachers of the Law and Pharisees! You hypocrites! You are like whitewashed tombs, which look fine on the outside but are full of bones and decaying corpses on the inside. In the same way, on the outside you appear good to everybody, but inside you are full of hypocrisy and sins."

MATT. 23:25–28

## Wineskins and Cloth

On one occasion the followers of John the Baptist and the Pharisees were fasting. Some people came to Jesus and asked him, "Why is it that the disciples of John the Baptist and the disciples of the Pharisees fast, but yours do not?"

Jesus answered, "Do you expect the guests at a wedding party to go without food? Of course not! As long as the bridegroom is with them, they will not do that. But the day will come when the bridegroom will be taken away from them, and then they will fast.

"No one uses a piece of new cloth to patch up an old coat, because the new patch will shrink and tear off some of the old cloth, making an even bigger hole. Nor does anyone pour new wine into used wineskins, because the wine will burst the skins, and both the wine and the skins will be ruined. Instead, new wine must be poured into fresh wineskins."

MARK 2:18-22

# Salt and Light

"You are like salt for all mankind. But if salt loses its saltiness, there is no way to make it salty again. It has become worthless, so it is thrown out and people trample on it.

"You are like light for the whole world. A city built on a hill cannot be hid. No one lights a lamp and puts it under a bowl; instead he puts it on the lampstand, where it gives light for everyone in the house. In the same way your light must shine before people, so that they will see the good things you do and praise your Father in heaven."

MATT. 5:13-16

# The Unmerciful Servant

Then Peter came to Jesus and asked, "Lord, if my brother keeps on sinning against me, how many times do I have to forgive him? Seven times?"

"No, not seven times," answered Jesus, "but seventy times seven, because the Kingdom of heaven is like this. Once there was a king who decided to check on his servants' accounts. He had just begun to do so when one of them was brought in who owed him millions of dollars. The servant did not have enough to pay his debt, so the king ordered him to be sold as a slave, with his wife and his children and all that he had, in order to pay the debt. The servant fell on his knees before the king. 'Be patient with me,' he begged, 'and I will pay you everything!' The king felt sorry for him, so he forgave him the debt and let him go.

"Then the man went out and met one of his fellow servants who owed him a few dollars. He grabbed him and started choking him. 'Pay back what you owe me!' he said. His fellow servant fell down and begged him, 'Be patient with me, and I will pay you back!' But he refused; instead, he had him thrown into jail until he should pay the debt. When the other servants saw what had happened, they were very upset and went to the king and told him everything. So he called the servant in. 'You worthless slave!' he said. 'I forgave you the whole amount you owed me, just because you asked me to. You should have had mercy on your fellow servant, just as I had mercy on you.' The king was very angry, and he sent the servant to jail to be punished until he should pay back the whole amount."

And Jesus concluded, "That is how my Father in heaven will treat every one of you unless you forgive your brother from your heart."

MATT. 18:21–35

# The Two Foundations

"So then, anyone who hears these words of mine and obeys them is like a wise man who built his house on rock. The rain poured down, the rivers flooded over, and the wind blew hard against that house. But it did not fall, because it was built on rock.

"But anyone who hears these words of mine and does not obey them is like a foolish man who built his house on sand. The rain poured down, the rivers flooded over, the wind blew hard against that house, and it fell. And what a terrible fall that was!"

When Jesus finished saying these things, the crowd was amazed at the way he taught. He wasn't like the teachers of the Law; instead, he taught with authority.

MATT. 7:24–29

**THEME FOUR**

# Purposeful Living
# Versus Just Getting By

## Introduction to the Modern Parables

Life is such an incredible, undeserved gift that it is horrible for us to waste any of it. But how can we *know* what is the best use for this gift and what is wasteful? What is life *for?* What are *we* for? When we get to the end of our lives and look back, with some kind of objectivity, what will we see as our best moments, our most worthwhile efforts? A great theologian once wrote that the way most of us spend our precious lives is like a jewelry store window which some vandal has smashed. Instead of stealing anything, he has simply—and mischievously—rearranged all the price tags so that the most valuable things have the cheapest prices and the least valuable things have the highest prices.

## *The Birdman of Wall Street*

Melvin, you must understand, was not an average man—although he looked like it. For Melvin had a secret life.

Every evening when Melvin came home from working as a book-keeper in a Wall Street accounting firm, he would take off his shiny blue serge coat and don a red velvet smoking jacket. He would gingerly take off his gold-framed spectacles and thrust a pair of bold horn-rims on his now-sparkling eyes. Then mild-mannered Melvin the bookkeeper would become Melvin the budgie expert. Thus transformed he would descend majestically into his basement, which was filled with the chirping, many-hued birdlets.

Here Melvin was king, for he now felt secure in the knowledge that no one in the world knew more than he did about budgies. For years he had read every book on budgie ornithology that had been written. Then, five years ago, he had begun writing his own book. It was to be the book about budgies to end all books about budgies. Many were the hours he had spent musing about the title which the book would have, but he always returned to his favorites—either the rather saucy *Compleat Budgie Lovers' Guide* or the simple but humble *Budgie Book.* Either title indicated the finality that Melvin knew his book would bring to the field.

You have no idea what immense satisfaction, what a glowing lamp of security was kept lit in Melvin's heart by his expertise. Often in his Wall Street office he would raise his head from his work, look over the nineteen other bowed and bald heads surrounding him, and smile his secret smile. It was his budgie-expert smile—the thing that made him different from, and far superior to, the other "Melvins" around him. If his work was not too pressing, he would have time for a small reverie in which he would usually see himself (a) retiring from the accounting firm after thirty-five years of exemplary service, (b) devoting himself full-time to budgie research and budgie writing, and then (c) having his book published and being invited all around the world to receive honors, make speeches, and be consulted on budgie problems.

Thus, Melvin was a happy man.

But almost without his being aware that it was going to happen, there was a party in the office one day. It was in Melvin's honor, in recognition of his thirty-five years of exemplary service to the accounting firm.

After the party, with confetti in his trouser cuffs and streamers trailing from his blue serge shoulders, Melvin went home. After looking through his smudgy budgie manuscript, he went out and sold his forty-seven budgies to a pet wholesaler for ninety-seven dollars and forty-three cents.

## Just Around the Corner

Eddie stood in his front yard and watched the big boys walking to school.

"When *I* get to be six I'll go to school, and it will be very nice," he said.

But when Eddie got to be six and did go to school, it wasn't all that nice.

"When I go to high school it'll be keen," Eddie said, dreaming of being a football star, driving his own jalopy, and having big muscles under his letter sweater.

But when Ed got to high school, things didn't work out the way he had planned.

"When I get out of this dumb place," he said with disgust, "I'm going to the University, where they treat you like an adult. It won't be boring, and the girls are too mature to care whether or not you're a football star."

The University didn't quite work out the way Ed planned either.

"Well," he said, "life is really going to begin when I graduate, get a good job, and have my own apartment."

But life didn't seem to get started too well, even when Ed found a pretty good job and had a much too expensive apartment all to himself.

"I'm so lonely," he said. "That's what's wrong. Just about everything that's wrong with my life now would be solved if I had a good wife."

Marriage did solve a lot of Ed's problems, but it created a few more—like money problems for instance.

"Just think how it'd be if I *got* that promotion," Ed chortled to his wife. "We could get a second car, go to Bermuda for our vacations, and even buy a house with a bedroom for each of the kids!"

But when Ed finally did get that promotion, the bigger income was soon swallowed up in bigger bills, and he was under just as much financial strain as ever. And with his new responsibilities he was under greater psychological pressure at the office. No, the promotion didn't make life happen.

"Life will really be wonderful," Edward mused as he looked searchingly at the gray at his temples in the mirror, "when I retire. I'll still be relatively young, and I can fish, hunt—be free of responsibilities."

Edward retired. He was out in his new boat one day, heading for a spot where the lodge's proprietor had assured him he'd have no trouble catching a six- or eight-pound bass.

"All my life I've been looking for happiness and contentment," he thought as the boat slid across the water. "When I get used to this retirement way of life, I think it's finally going to be great!"

Of course, by now he didn't really believe that. That's why he added (to reassure himself), "Now, for the first time, I feel that life—*real living*—is just around the corner!"

With a searing pain in his chest, Edward turned that corner. And there it was, waiting for him. No, not life—death.

With that he dropped the whole matter.

# The Fatstock Show

Two young men went to the State Fair one day. They were somewhat frustrated to find that the two major events of the day were scheduled simultaneously. Undaunted, they agreed to split up, one to each event, and then to give detailed accounts of the events to each other afterward. That way neither one would miss much.

Two hours later they met at the hot dog stand to compare notes.

"How did your event begin?"

"The band played as a long line of very fine cattle were led into the arena for the people to see. Each was a prime example of its species and had been washed and brushed until it fairly gleamed."

"Mine began the same way, with but a single difference. Then what happened?"

"Each animal was paraded in front of a panel of judges who noted the texture of its hide; the condition of its eyes, teeth, and gums; and its weight and proportions."

"My event was just the same at that point. Go on."

"After the judges had looked at all the cattle, they put their heads together and chose the one which was the finest of its breed, and, amidst large applause from the audience, they put a blue ribbon around the neck of the winner."

"Exactly what happened at my event! What happened to the winner?"

"Oh. That was a very macabre thing. After being selected the finest of its breed, receiving thunderous accolades, being showered with prizes, after being led to the heights of glory . . ."

"Yes?"

"It was led off to be destroyed by some of the very people who had been so enraptured by its excellence of form."

"Alas, that's how my event probably ended too."

"That is strange. Did you go to a Fatstock Show too?"

"No, I went to the Beauty Contest."

"Oh, yes. That's right."

# The Man Who
# Feared His Neighbors

A certain young farmer found that trying to work a small farm was no longer a way to make a good living for his family, so he moved the family to the suburbs and took a job in a factory.

The ex-farmer was surprised at how easily he was able to make the transition from working on the farm to working in the factory. What really bothered him most about his move was having neighbors living so closely to him on both sides, behind him, and facing his house across the street. When he was at home he felt closed in, trapped, surrounded.

One evening as he sat on his front porch in the deepening gloom, he thought thus to himself: "How different it used to be on the farm. I could look for miles in any direction and not even see smoke from a chimney. But now I can't look fifty feet without seeing someone else's house, someone else's car, someone else's kids!"

This situation bothered him greatly, but he was not quite sure why until one day it occurred to him. "I'm afraid!" he whispered to himself. "That feeling I've been having since we moved here—it's fear! But of what?"

He thought about this for a few more days, and then suddenly realized that it was his neighbors of whom he was afraid. Their very closeness was a threat to him.

"I'm always reading about some city fellow going berserk and shooting his own family, then turning the gun on his neighbors," he thought. "If one of our neighbors should do this, there'd be no place to run, no place to hide. I couldn't even protect my own family!"

Shuddering with this thought, he ran to the shopping center to buy himself a pistol and two boxes of shells.

Now, whenever he looked at his neighbors, he was unconsciously looking for signs of hostility from them. And he always saw what he was looking for. One day the neighbor on his left was mowing his lawn and maliciously cut two swaths out of the ex-farmer's lawn. Another day the right-hand neighbor's kids deliberately rolled their ball across his lawn. On yet another day the top to one of his garbage cans mysteriously wound up on one of the garbage cans of his neighbor across the alley.

Becoming more and more agitated and frightened by such overt acts of hostility, the ex-farmer ran again to the shopping center, this time to buy a shotgun, a rifle with telescopic sights, and an emergency supply of shells and cartridges.

Upon his return home, he did not fail to notice that some of his neighbors were spying at his packages through their curtains, and others were openly grimacing at him from their yards. Under cover of the hedges, he ran into his house and locked and barricaded the doors.

So frightened that he could hardly breathe or talk, he ordered his family not to go outdoors or even show themselves at the windows.

He kept his family barricaded in their house for four days, waiting for the attack which he was sure was going to come from his neighbors. All this time he was feeling more and more hopeless about their chances of getting out of the situation alive. Even if he were able to shoot a few of them, there were far more neighbors than he could hope to stand off for long. And if he were killed or captured, he shuddered to think of what would happen to his wife and daughters at the hands of those vicious, inhuman neighbors.

Crouching to peer through the blinds, nervously fingering the trigger on his shotgun, the ex-farmer grew more and more afraid. His fear became a thick fog which rose to cloud his eyes, his mind.

On the fifth day the front page of the newspapers carried stories, with pictures, about a suburban man who had gone berserk, shot and killed members of his own family, then turned his gun on his neighbors.

# Too Much,
## Too Little, Too Late

Flora faced herself in the mirror. She hated what she saw—fat.

She closed her eyes. "Oh, God," she breathed, "make the new pills work. Don't let me be fat anymore. Don't. Being fat is the worst thing in the world."

Mei-Li found some grubs beneath a rock. Hurriedly she scratched them up and ate them, getting as much dirt as grubs in her mouth. It was no matter—the dirt would fill her stomach too. The grubs only made the dirt go down easier.

"If I only had some salt, just a little bit of salt," frowned Mei-Li, "then the grubs would go down easier and I would be happy."

Mrs. Foster looked at the cellophane-wrapped meat and asked, "Is this fresh? I mean *really* fresh?"

"Yes, ma'am. Sure it is. I just cut it this afternoon," the butcher assured her.

Picking out a six-pound roast, Mrs. Foster put it in her cart and continued her rounds of the supermarket aisles, between stacks of canned and boxed foods, fruits, and vegetables.

"Three dollars for a pound of seven-rib roast," she muttered to herself. "Outrageous! We've had to give up eating steak already! Humph! Somebody would make a million on a cookbook called *One Hundred Ways to Serve Hamburger. I'd* surely buy it!"

Sighing, she continued to load up her cart, dreading the numbers which would pop up in the little window of the cash register.

Marebi-Gabo doled out the grain to the women—a double handful for each house. He had learned to look at the eyes and not down at the swollen bellies—especially of the little ones. Although he was embarrassed to be giving so little grain into the eager hands, he was still thankful that there was enough grain left in the village storehouse—perhaps enough so that each person would have at least a cake each day until those green shoots in the fields matured and produced more. They would be all right then, if it didn't rain too much or too little, or if the river didn't overflow its banks, or if the insects didn't come, or if . . .

Jimmy didn't cry very often. You don't if you're thirteen years old. But this was the worst day of his life, and of all his friends he was surely the most unfortunate, neglected, and deprived. His eyes filled with tears again, and his throat ached to cry aloud as he sat on the bed in his room, hearing again his father's harsh words, "No! And don't ask me again! You can't have a motor bike until *next* year when you're fourteen, and that's *final!*"

## Better to Have Loved?

Once there were two brothers. The older brother had a very good friend with whom he spent much of his time. For several years the two friends went everywhere and did everything together. In so doing they shared many confidences. But one day the older brother's friend refused his offer to go to the movies, and on the next day the "friend" proclaimed publicly some confidences of the older brother that were very injurious, and exposed the older brother to ridicule and scorn.

It was a great comfort to the older brother, hurt and now very lonely, to find a quiet and rather attractive young woman with whom he could share his time, his concerns, his life. For several months they had an idyllic existence, finding great fulfillment in each other. But then the young woman found someone she liked better and drifted out of the older brother's life.

The older brother thereupon resolved that he would never again open up his life to another person. That seemed to him the only way to avoid the deep pain which he had already experienced twice.

The younger brother's experience was not so different from that of the elder. He too was betrayed by a friend and exposed to public scorn; he too was rejected by a young woman he had loved very deeply. But even in the midst of the pain and sorrow of his broken friendships and forsaken loves, he always reached out for another friend, another love.

One day the elder brother spoke quite seriously to the younger. "Look here," he said, "why do you expose yourself to such pain, such sorrow? You have been betrayed, neglected, and even viciously beaten by your so-called friends—not just once, but many times. And not content with the sorrow of one lost love, you were heartbroken by many lost loves in your courting days. Now you are married. But one child died and the one who lives is retarded. And I see, when I visit you two, how often you and your wife argue and fight, what agony you give each other—*much* more than you'd ever dream of venting on mere strangers! Why have you gone on this way when you could have been safe from such pain, even as I have been these peaceful years of mine?"

But the younger brother was unable to give any answer that made much sense to the elder.

## Introduction to the Biblical Parables

Jesus, in many of his parables, invites us to think about and to examine very carefully our concepts of what life is really about. He challenges us to think about the vast difference between living in the off-hand, relatively aimless "way of the world" and the kind of existence that begins here and now as living in the "Kingdom of God."

## *The Hidden Treasure/The Pearl*

"The Kingdom of heaven is like this. A man happens to find a treasure hidden in a field. He covers it up again, and is so happy that he goes and sells everything he has, and then goes back and buys that field.

"Also, the Kingdom of heaven is like this. A man is looking for fine pearls, and when he finds one that is unusually fine, he goes and sells everything he has, and buys that pearl."

MATT. 13:44–46

## *The Unprepared Servant*

"Who, then, is a faithful and wise servant? He is the one that his master has placed in charge of the other servants to give them their food at the proper time. How happy that servant is if his master finds him doing this when he comes home! Indeed, I tell you, the master will put that servant in charge of all his property. But if he is a bad servant, he will tell himself that his master will not come back for a long time, and he will begin to beat his fellow servants and to eat and drink with drunkards. Then that servant's master will come back one day when the servant does not expect him and at a time he does not know. The master will cut him in pieces and make him share the fate of the hypocrites. There he will cry and gnash his teeth."

MATT. 24:45–51

# The Rich Fool

A man in the crowd said to Jesus, "Teacher, tell my brother to divide with me the property our father left us."

Jesus answered him, "Man, who gave me the right to judge or to divide the property between you two?" And he went on to say to them all, "Watch out and guard yourselves from every kind of greed; because a person's true life is not made up of the things he owns, no matter how rich he may be."

Then Jesus told them this parable: "There was once a rich man who had land which bore good crops. He began to think to himself, 'I don't have a place to keep all my crops. What can I do? This is what I will do,' he told himself; 'I will tear down my barns and build bigger ones, where I will store the grain and all my other goods. Then I will say to myself, Lucky man! You have all the good things you need for many years. Take life easy, eat, drink, and enjoy yourself!' But God said to him, 'You fool! This very night you will have to give up your life; then who will get all these things you have kept for yourself?' "

And Jesus concluded, "This is how it is with those who pile up riches for themselves but are not rich in God's sight."

LUKE 12:13–21

# The Rich Man and Lazarus

"There was once a rich man who dressed in the most expensive clothes and lived in great luxury every day. There was also a poor man named Lazarus, covered with sores, who used to be brought to the rich man's door, hoping to eat the bits of food that fell from the rich man's table. Even the dogs would come and lick his sores. The poor man died and was carried by the angels to sit beside Abraham at the feast in heaven.

The rich man died and was buried, and in Hades, where he was in great pain, he looked up and saw Abraham, far away, with Lazarus at his side. So he called out, 'Father Abraham! Take pity on me, and send Lazarus to dip his finger in some water and cool off my tongue, because I am in great pain in this fire!' But Abraham said, 'Remember, my son, that in your lifetime you were given all the good things, while Lazarus got all the bad things. But now he is enjoying himself here, while you are in pain. Besides all that, there is a deep pit lying between us, so that those who want to cross over from here to you cannot do so, nor can anyone cross over to us from where you are.' The rich man said, 'Then I beg you, father Abraham, send Lazarus to my father's house, where I have five brothers. Let him go and warn them so that they, at least, will not come to this place of pain.' Abraham said, 'Your brothers have Moses and the prophets to warn them; your brothers should listen to what they say.' The rich man answered, 'That is not enough, father Abraham! But if someone were to rise from death and go to them, then they would turn from their sins.' But Abraham said, 'If they will not listen to Moses and the prophets, they will not be convinced even if someone were to rise from death.'"

LUKE 16:19-31

## The Gold Coins

While the people were listening to this, Jesus continued and told them a parable. He was now almost at Jerusalem, and they supposed that the Kingdom of God was just about to appear. So he said, "There was once a man of high rank who was going to a country far away to be made king, after which he planned to come back home. Before he left, he called his ten servants and gave them each a gold coin and told them, 'See what you can earn with this while I am gone.' Now, his countrymen hated him, and so they sent messengers after him to say, 'We don't want this man to be our king.'

"The man was made king and came back. At once he ordered his servants to appear before him, in order to find out how much they had earned. The first one came and said, 'Sir, I have earned ten gold coins with the one you gave me.' 'Well done,' he said; 'you are a good servant! Since you were faithful in small matters, I will put you in charge of ten cities.' The second servant came and said, 'Sir, I have earned five gold coins with the one you gave me.' To this one he said, 'You will be in charge of five cities.' Another servant came and said, 'Sir, here is your gold coin; I kept it hidden in a handkerchief. I was afraid of you, because you are a hard man. You take what is not yours and reap what you did not plant.' He said to him, 'You bad servant! I will use your own words to condemn you! You know that I am a hard man, taking what is not mine and reaping what I have not planted. Well, then, why didn't you put my money in the bank? Then I would have received it back with interest when I returned.' Then he said to those who were standing there, 'Take the gold coin away from him and give it to the servant who has ten coins.' But they said to him, 'Sir, he already has ten coins!' 'I tell you,' he replied, 'that to every person who has something, even more will be given; but the person who has nothing, even the little that he has will be taken away from him. Now, as for those enemies of mine who did not want me to be their king, bring them here and kill them in my presence!' "

LUKE 19:11–27

# Suggested Questions for Thought and Discussion

For those who read this book by themselves, the following questions are offered as possible helps to private ruminations. For those who read this book as part of a group study and discussion program, the following questions are offered in hope that they can help a group use the parables as springboards to fruitful discussion.

Wherever a question has several parts ("What do you think of the priest's habits and attitudes? The hermit's?"), it is intended that the questions should be dealt with separately, rather than all at once.

The author offers these questions with important reservations, realizing that many persons and groups will find them unnecessary and that the questions coming from group members themselves are usually far more appropriate than any "canned" questions might be.

# Introduction

### The Man Who Would Communicate (pp. 8–12)

1. What the young teacher discovered in the garden is attested to by Henry J. Cadbury, who wrote, "The facts of religion and of ethics may be directly observed in nature and in men since all of life is homogeneous and mutually analogous." What are some of the "homogeneous and mutually analogous" elements you have discovered which illuminate religion and ethics?

2. Why did the young teacher leap to the assumption that he needed to "boil down" his illuminative experience into propositions and concepts before he could pass it on? Is this a popular conception of communicators today? How effective is it?

3. What do you think of the teacher's recognition that making abstractions from concrete experiences, drawing the explicit truth

from implicit situations, is the work of the learner rather than of the teacher?

4. Why were there such varied reactions to the young teacher's parables? See if the experience of Jesus with his parables (Matt. 13:10-15) throws any light on the question.

5. If ours is predominantly a "visually oriented" rather than a "linearly oriented" culture today (because of the high incidence of screen communication), do you agree that the "visual language" of parables might have a better communicative power than straight address? Why or why not?

6. Since a parable can be interpreted in several different ways, rather than imposing one "correct" interpretation upon its hearers, is it a viable teaching tool? Why or why not?

7. Why do we usually assume that abstract speech is the most viable form of communication?

8. Would it be possible for a good teacher to set up experiences for his or her students, from which they could draw their own learning? What kinds of experiences could be used for this purpose?

9. Have you ever noticed how difficult—or impossible—it is to simply "hand over" a truth to someone else? Why must they learn it for themselves, when they could save so much time and trouble simply by taking your word for it?

## THEME ONE: Mission Versus Institution

### The Village That Forgot (pp. 15–16)

1. What did you think of the rich man's decision to provide food, clothing, and shelter for every person in the village?

2. Should the rich man first have done a survey to determine if there was an even more needy village? Why or why not?

3. How did the villagers feel when their support funds were cut in half and then cut again? Do you think that is the usual reaction people have to such a situation? How would you explain their reaction?

4. Does a gift still seem like a gift when a person becomes accustomed to it?

5. How do we fall into the habit of taking that which we have not earned "for granted" or as our "due"? Why is it that we behave as if we *deserve* or have *earned* or can *expect* one more morning, one

more year of life, our next breath, or a gesture of love or friendship? How would we and our lives be different if we didn't?

6. How do we react when such gifts stop coming or are cut back?
7. If you were the rich man, how would you have reacted when the villagers stoned your messenger and then looted and burned your home? What would you have done?
8. If you were God, and even the best of your world's folk treated your gifts as if they were *due* them on a day-to-day basis, what would you do?
9. What would be the best way to restore a sense of givenness to an accustomed gift? What could the giver do? What could the receiver do?
10. What is there about the virtue of gratitude that makes it so rare and short-lived? Do we grow to resent the giver upon whom we come to depend? Do we feel that receiving becomes demeaning?

## The Mislaid Mission (pp. 17–18)

1. If the Church is "like a mighty army," is it true that we too sometimes forget what our mission is? What are some forms of churchly activity that proliferate when this forgetting happens?
2. What of the sergeant who imagined their mission was to exterminate all the flies? Could a mighty institution—like a church or a nation—fall into using its powers merely to perform relatively unimportant tasks or just to remove some of those things that irritate its members?
3. What did the active sergeant imagine that he was defending? What happens when zealous defensiveness is based on vague grounds?
4. Can vagueness or disagreement about objective and mission lead to self-destruction within a church or a nation? How can the *real* mission be discovered, clarified, and agreed upon?
5. If Jesus or Peter or Paul were to come to your church to see how their efforts were being carried on today, what things would you show them? What things might you try to hide?
6. When your church is most definitely and unmistakably fulfilling its God-given mission, what is it doing? How does it feel to participate in that mission?
7. If we were to accept that "preparation" covers everything Christians do within the walls of their church building, and that "mission" is that which is done outside in the world, what is your church's mission this week? What forms of preparation should be going on?

8. What needs to happen in order for a church or any other large institution to accomplish its mission? Does success depend on the participation of all its members? Why or why not?
9. What can an individual do to clarify his or her own mission in life? How might such clarification affect the person's daily living?

## Lying Offshore (pp. 19–21)

1. Why were the people on the ship so vague about the initial purpose of their voyage? How could they possibly have come to the conclusion that all the ship's provisions were for *them?*
2. Did studying the logbook seem to help the passengers? Why not?
3. Why were most of the passengers reluctant to go ashore?
4. Who—or what—was the old man to the rest of the ship's crew and passengers? What was his function? Why was he unsuccessful?
5. Why did a few of the younger men and women go ashore? Why were they listed as "lost at sea"?
6. Why did the supplies begin to molder? What will happen to the people still on the ship? The people on the shore?
7. The Church itself has often been likened to a ship. What kinds of likenesses can you discern?
8. What is likely to happen to a very long-term mission, which is passed on from generation to generation? How can its goals be kept sharp and the missioners' enthusiasm strong?
9. Is it possible that your church could arrive at the point it was created to serve, and not know it? What might some of those points be?
10. How can the referral of matters to a committee be simply a way of avoiding a decision? How could the committee actually have led the ship to fulfillment of its mission?

## The Image Behind the Image (pp. 22–23)

1. What, if anything, was wrong with putting the image of Tlaloc behind the image of the Virgin, if it brought such desirable results?
2. Why is a full house of worship traditionally such a much-desired thing?
3. Do the appearances of institutional success ever mask the essential failure of a church? Might a truly successful church present outward appearances of failure?
4. What motivations seem to have driven the priest to adopt such

means to numerical success? What are some other means to numerical and financial success that might be used today?

5. And what about the old *cacique*? Are there other instances in which a person or group may divert the purposes of an institution to their own ends, while leaving the institution appearing outwardly the same?

6. How do you feel about the Conquistadores' efforts to destroy the Aztecs' religion in order to establish their own faith in the Aztecs' land?

7. What is the difference between "evangelism" and "religious imperialism"?

8. If the situation were reversed, and your religion was the one being persecuted, would you go into the temple of Tlaloc to worship if a cross or a holy image was secreted behind the idol? Why or why not?

9. What do you think of Father Anselmo's attempts at evangelism by using promises of better crop yields for converts to his religion?

10. Will the old *cacique* go down in history as a friend or an enemy to his own religion? Why?

## The Sacred Priest and the Profane Hermit (pp. 24–26)

1. What do you think of the priest's habits and attitudes? The hermit's?

2. What are the contrasts between the hermit's idea of "ministry to the world" and the priest's?

3. Is there any need for those who would minister to the world to consider contemporary poetry, plays, fiction, movies, and magazines? Why or why not?

4. Does the Jesus presented to us in the Gospels immerse himself more intimately into his culture than the Church of today does? Does the Church seem to you to be "largely aloof"?

5. Was the priest justified before God by his efforts? Why or why not?

6. Was the hermit justified by his confession? Why or why not?

7. What was the difference between the attitudes of the priest and those of the hermit? Was the priest truly "sacred" and the hermit really "profane"? Explain your answer.

8. What do you think about the priest labeling the hermit's books and magazines as "pornography"? Why would he do that?

9. Did you think that the hermit was overly humble to the priest? Should he have stood up for himself more? Could he have taught the priest a thing or two about honesty and true religion?

10. What do you think of the Church speaking to the world through such "worldly" channels as television, movies, or even comic books?

### The Sower (p. 27)

1. How would you characterize a modern-day experience of someone who was like the first condition—hearing the word, but immediately having it taken away?
2. How about the seed that "fell on rocky ground"? Make up a short, short story about someone like that.
3. What are some of the "thorns" or "weeds" that can grow up in our lives and choke out the Word, so that it bears no fruit in us?
4. What, in your own terms, does it mean today to "bear fruit" from the seed of the Word of God?

### The Wicked Tenants (p. 28)

1. What emotions do you have as you read this parable?
2. Do you think that your emotional response was the one Jesus desired from his hearers? Why did he want his hearers to have such a response?
3. In your own words, and as briefly as possible, state what you think is the main point of this parable.
4. How does the scripture which Jesus cited relate to the main point?

### The Great Supper (pp. 28–29)

1. In terms of our own lives here and now, what does it mean to be invited to the "great supper," but to make excuses and refuse to come?
2. What does the parable mean by saying that our places at the supper will be taken by others?
3. Look again at the three "apologies" used by those who refused to come to the supper. What quality or qualities do they all have in common?

### The Good Samaritan (pp. 29–30)

1. The "teacher of the Law" had just heard the Great Commandment about loving your neighbor as you love yourself, and wanted to know how many people, or what kinds of people, he was supposed to love. What was his answer from Jesus?

2. What is Jesus' definition of *neighbor* here? How far does our own "neighborhood" extend?
3. What did Jesus mean by using a priest and a Levite as bad examples, and a Samaritan as the good example? How would you restate these examples in modern terms?

### The Pharisee and the Tax Collector (p. 30)

1. The Pharisee has obviously tried very hard to live by religious rules, while the tax collector apparently has not. Why, then, isn't the Pharisee the one who is "right with God"?
2. What did the sinner (the tax collector) do which made him "right with God"? What was his attitude, as contrasted with the Pharisee's?
3. What does this parable say to us about our pride in tithing, bringing people to church, avoiding some sins, or doing good works?

# THEME TWO: Love Versus Bargaining

### A Bargain with God (pp. 33–35)

1. What do you think of Simon Pure's "bargain with God"? Was it biblical, as he claimed it was?
2. Had Penny Poor done any more or less to *deserve* God's blessings than Simon Pure had? Are such things as financial success rightly called "blessings of God"?
3. Why had Simon been more successful than Penny? Did it have anything to do with Simon's having made a bargain or with Penny's not having made one?
4. What was Simon's reaction when his store burned down? Is this the fate of all who create for themselves a god with whom they can bargain?
5. What is the relationship of the death of an idol like Simon's to the "Death of God" controversy?
6. Many evangelists have based their ministries upon the lure of earthly—or even heavenly—rewards, sometimes along with the threats of punishment here or hereafter. What do you think of such pleasure-pain appeals, or appeals to greed and fear? What was Jesus' way of appealing?
7. Simon used his religion aggressively as a tool in his business. Was Penny missing something by not doing this, too?

8. If you were God, how would you rate Simon and Penny, relatively, as "deserving"? Why did Simon prosper while Penny failed? Why did Simon's faith collapse while Penny's remained strong?
9. Was Simon's success from God, viewed as God's keeping His half of the bargain? Was the fire from God? How about the rain—or even the Tower of Siloam—which seems to fall upon both the just and the unjust, according to Jesus?

## The Just Merchant (pp. 36-37)

1. What does it mean when all people are equal, and yet "some are more equal than others" (with thanks to George Orwell's *Animal Farm*)?
2. Did you agree or disagree with the merchants' opinion that it is bad for government to tell private businesses whom to hire? Why?
3. What about the statement, "You can't legislate morals anyway"? If this is true, does it mean that no legislation affecting moral problems should be considered? *Was* this only a moral problem?
4. What did you think of the merchant's way of controlling employment practices "on the local level"?
5. What did you think of his peers' response to his action? Is it right to discriminate against discriminators?
6. Do you know of any instances of sexual discrimination in employment practices? Describe them.
7. Do you know of any instances of racial discrimination in employment practices? Describe them.
8. Do you know of any instances of religious discrimination in employment practices? Describe them.
9. What would be some instances of age discrimination in employment practices?
10. Should such discriminatory practices be stopped, or do employers have a right to be as discriminating as they like?

## Jake and Easy (pp. 38-39)

1. Which son seemed to care most for his father? Were the appearances misleading?
2. What do you think of Jake's business policies—the general policy of "let the buyer beware"?
3. What do you think of Easy's avoidance of involvement in "the establishment" and his activities among his neighbors?

4. Do you find yourself more sympathetic with Jake or with Easy? If not with either of them, what do you think can be done to help create a better way which corrects the problem of poverty without going to either extreme?

5. In the sixties, Jake would have looked to everyone like a "straight" and Easy like a "hippie." How would the way such men dress be different today, two decades later? What does such an outward difference signify to the casual observer?

6. Should a father expect his children to carry on a family-owned business? Why or why not?

7. What seems to be Jake's attitude toward his fellow man? Easy's attitude?

8. How would it be possible for two sons of the same father to have such radically different attitudes?

9. Do you know of such unethical business practices in your community? What would you do about them if you did?

10. What would you think of someone who "fronted" for a minority family with a real estate agent so that they could move into a neighborhood otherwise closed to them?

## The Children (pp. 40–41)

1. Why were the older brother and sisters suddenly so attentive to their father?

2. If you had been the ailing father, how would you have felt about your older children's sudden attentiveness after years of neglect?

3. How was Edward different from the others? Why was this difference interpreted by them as a lack of love for his father?

4. If you had been Edward, what might you have said to your brother and sisters?

5. How did you respond to the father's final pronouncement about his children? Was he fair or loving to make such a statement?

6. How do you feel about the father's final statement? Could a father have loveless children and not be partially to blame himself?

7. How would the older brother and sisters have behaved if they had loved their father for himself, rather than for what they hoped he would give them?

8. Is it loving to serve and obey God only in order to win peace of mind or treasures in heaven, or to escape hell? How is "loving God for himself" different from "loving" God for what we hope to get out of him?

9. John Calvin asked his aspiring preachers whether they would be willing to be condemned eternally to hell if they were sure that their condemnation would serve to glorify God. How might you have answered? What would a "no" answer signify? A "yes" answer?

## The Two Magistrates (pp. 42–43)

1. Do you feel that the magistrate made the right decision in his effort to help the woman? Why or why not?
2. Do you agree or disagree with the other magistrate that simply giving the woman a free income might push her further into her problem?
3. What might have been the best way for the magistrate to act responsibly toward the woman?
4. What did the ruling magistrate reveal about his attitude toward the woman (and others in her circumstances) with his last remarks? Do you agree or disagree with his attitude?
5. If you had been the woman, how would you have felt about the judge's actions toward you?
6. If you committed some crime or error, which of these magistrates would you rather have as your judge? Why?
7. Can you identify any social reform movements which seem insensitive to the feelings of dignity and self-esteem of those they seek to help?
8. Is there much genuine altruism—completely selfless service for the benefit of others—or is much of it merely a way for us to get respect, "a larger mansion in heaven," or publicity? Why did Jesus say for us not to let our right hand know what the left hand was doing in such circumstances?
9. What are some of the "sins of altruism" of which we may be guilty as we take our Christmas baskets to the poor, send our cast-off books and clothes to missionaries, and so forth?
10. How would you deal with the awesome responsibility for deciding a person's guilt or innocence and how he or she should be punished? What qualities does such a responsibility demand?

## The Laborers in the Vineyard (pp. 44–45)

1. How would you have felt if you had worked from dawn to dark and received a certain agreed-upon sum, but found that the person who began working just before dark was getting the same pay?

2. What, to you, is the main point of this parable? What if the main point was how you responded when you were called, rather than how much work you did? Who would be deserving of the pay under those circumstances?
3. How does this parable relate to the one about the Pharisee and the tax collector (p. 30)?

## The Two Sons (p. 45)

1. What is a modern way of saying "Yes, sir!" but then not going to work?
2. What does it mean for Jesus to tell us that "tax collectors and prostitutes" are going into the Kingdom of God before those who say "Yes, sir!" but don't go to work?
3. What was the "right path" which John the Baptist showed?

## The Prodigal Son (pp. 45–46)

1. How would you have felt if you had been the older son? Why would it have been wrong for you to feel that way?
2. Why did Jesus tell so many parables about those who *expect* good things but do not receive them, while the good things are given to those who did *not* expect them? What are some of those other parables?
3. How do these "parables of expectation" apply to us, in our day?

# THEME THREE: Grace Versus the Law

## The Innovator (pp. 49–51)

1. Projecting the world-as-it-is into the future several decades, can you see innovation becoming a crime? If so, what kinds of innovation might be most harshly punished?
2. What, to you, is the central point of this parable?
3. What usually happens to innovators in your church, your business, your community, your school?
4. Can you recount the stories of some innovators in history and how they were received?
5. What is so threatening to many persons about the new, the different, and that which casts a critical eye upon the old and traditional?

6. What has to happen to a society, a group, or even an individual before innovation and challenge can be accepted with openness rather than fear and defensiveness?
7. How would you characterize the position of Christianity relative to innovation? Of democracy? You might contrast the "ideal" positions with the "actual" positions.
8. How do any of us become "set in our ways" when change is such an ever-present fact of modern existence?
9. How do we decide what is worth hanging on to or fighting for and what is not?
10. Why did the city fathers paint the dome opaquely all around and then publish false accounts of the Innovator's death?

## The Educated Medicine Man (pp. 52–53)

1. Why was tradition more dear than healing to Mwambo's people? Is this a widespread attitude? What else might be less important than tradition to some persons?
2. Can you cite some instances in our society in which it seems that people prefer old and obviously inadequate ways to new and more effective ways? Why does this happen?
3. Would it have been better for Mwambo never to have gone to Johns Hopkins? Better for whom?
4. What made Mwambo decide to go to Johns Hopkins in the first place, rather than simply to continue the practices of his ancestors?
5. If you had been Mwambo, returning to face rejection, how might you have acted differently?
6. What would be a parallel to Mwambo's decision in your own life? In your community? In your church?
7. What happens to young, vigorous leaders with new ideas when they are rejected and ridiculed by those they attempt to serve? What happens to a church or a society which rejects and ridicules new ideas, new ways, new leaders?
8. How might you be received if you went away for training and came back to change things?
9. How might your church or your city council be received if it set out, bravely and strongly, to change some old ways that seemed harmful?

## The Diamond (pp. 54–55)

1. How could the prospector have proved the superiority of his rough,

uncut stone over the shiny, faceted glass, especially to a group of persons who seemed never to have heard of a diamond? If proof was not possible, did this mean that the glass *was* more valuable?

2. How does something become valuable in a society—by consensus of the citizens or by something intrinsic to the thing itself? What if the question concerns not a thing, but an abstract value such as love or truth? Are values self-evident, self-authenticating, or must their value be demonstrated?

3. How could a society dedicated to the memory and values of the dead prospector erect a monument embodying the antithesis of his values?

4. After the prospector was killed, what do you suppose happened to make a few people decide that he had been right?

5. Why were the prospector's disciples unable, apparently, finally to change anything in the Great Glass City?

6. Why were the once-hated followers of the dead prospector called "glass-haters" rather than "diamond-lovers"?

7. The rough, uncut diamond didn't *look* as pretty as the polished glass. When was the last time you tried to convince someone (or perhaps yourself) that a rough virtue was more valuable than a pretty vice? What happened?

8. When an entire society or city or group seems united in prizing something inferior over something superior, how can the situation be changed? Can you give a modern example of such a change?

9. Taking your town or city as an example, what is the chief form of "glass worship"? What, in contrast, would be the "diamond-value"?

10. The late Archbishop William Temple compared prevailing value systems to a jewelry store which had been broken into by a mischievous vandal who had stolen nothing, but switched the price tags on the most expensive items to the cheapest items, and vice versa. Does this seem true to you as a critique of our contemporary value systems? If so, what are some specific examples?

## Creatures of Habit (pp. 56–57)

1. Why were the animals outside, freezing, rather than inside, enjoying the comfort of their new barn?

2. We may laugh at the silly animals, but are we so unlike them after all? Can you cite some ways in which we have done similar things?

3. Why are some of us so afraid of change that we will suffer to avoid it and even to keep others from experiencing it?

4. Have you ever heard of a congregation that split up because some wanted to stay in the small, old building while others wanted to move to a new, larger building? How would this be similar to the parable? How would it be different?
5. What do you think of the farmer's reasons for building the new barn?
6. Is there some habit you have which may be keeping you from occupying a better position in life? Why do you still have it?
7. What is the difference between good habits and bad habits? Can a good habit become a bad one, or a bad habit be mistaken for a good one? Think of examples.
8. Habits may be described as "patterns of behavior which, once set, are usually repeated without conscious deliberation." Are there parts of our lives which we should guard against habit-setting? Like what, for instance?

### Confession Is Good for the Cell (pp. 58–59)

1. Is there something of Hymie in all of us? Why is it so hard for us to admit guilt, even when it is very evident? How do you usually handle your guilt?
2. Is it possible for a guilty person to persuade himself (if not others) that he is innocent? What if he is guilty, not of some outward crime, but of subtler vices like prejudice, selfishness, closed-mindedness, or arrogance?
3. Christian tradition holds that false protestation of innocence condemns the sinner to a repetition of his sins. He is trapped, imprisoned by them. Do you find this to be true in terms of your own experience or not?
4. On the other hand, a traditional Christian concept of confession is that it releases the sinner from his sin, absolves him so that he is free from it. Do you find this to be true in your own experience or not?
5. Is accepting the truth about one's self actually as dramatically "freeing" as Hymie's experience was? What are some of the "prisons" we can be freed from by sincere confession?
6. Hymie knew he was guilty all along, so why did he claim innocence and even feel self-righteous? Is self-righteousness often (or always) built upon deep-seated guilt feelings?
7. What is the Protestant equivalent of confession, and how does it work?

8. Is a general confession of sin effective enough to free us from our guilt, or must the confession be very specific in order to be effective?
9. In criminal justice, the offender can often receive a lighter sentence by admitting his guilt and "throwing himself upon the mercy of the court." What is the spiritual equivalent for this action?

## Woes to the Pharisees (p. 60)
1. What are some ways we have of cleaning the outside of the cup while the inside remains dirty?
2. What might be some of the "whitewashed tombs" among us today?

## Wineskins and Cloth (pp. 60–61)
1. What, in Jesus' view, was the relationship of feasting and fasting?
2. What, in Jesus' view, was the relationship between the old and the new?
3. How do these views of Jesus apply to our individual and church lives?

## Salt and Light (p. 61)
1. What does it mean to be "salt"? To lose our "saltiness"? How does salt function, anyway?
2. What does it mean for us to be "light"? To hide our "light"?

## The Unmerciful Servant (pp. 61–62)
1. It must strike us all as outrageous and unthinkable that a person who has just been forgiven a debt of millions of dollars would turn around and put another person in jail over a debt of only a few dollars, but what if God let us live one more day and we awoke still holding a grudge against someone? Wouldn't that be the same? How would it be the same or different?
2. If we do not forgive others, what is the punishment that Jesus promises us?
3. To Peter's question of how far he must go in forgiving someone who has sinned against him, what was Jesus' answer?

## The Two Foundations (p. 62)
1. What would it mean for you to "build your house upon sand"?

2. How can you "build your house upon rock"? What does that mean, in very practical, everyday terms?

## THEME FOUR: Purposeful Living Versus Just Getting By

### The Birdman of Wall Street (pp. 65–66)

1. Upon what did Melvin base his life? Was this a well-founded basis?
2. Did Melvin's involvement with the budgies prevent him from finding meaning in his work as an accountant? What should have been the relationship of his vocation to his avocation?
3. Why was his retirement such a blow to Melvin, when he had apparently looked forward to it for years?
4. Why did Melvin sell his birds? What will become of him now? How might he have avoided this fate?
5. Using Melvin as an example, illustrate why we talk of pride as a vice, and of humility as a virtue.
6. Is being a bookkeeper inherently less noble than being an ornithological expert? Are some jobs more noble than others?
7. What is the difference between a corporation president and a street cleaner who does his work with joy and dedication? Should we respect one more than another? Why or why not?
8. Do you find fulfillment in your daily work, your chosen vocation (while you're in school, by the way, your vocation is being a student)?

### Just Around the Corner (pp. 67–68)

1. What was Ed waiting for?
2. Why did Ed think that waiting would bring about "real life"? Could he have done anything himself to bring it about? What?
3. Why did he always despise the condition he was in and spend his time longing for a condition he hoped was to come?
4. What do you think of "just-around-the-corner-ism" as a way of life? Do you practice it?
5. What seems to you to be the central point which Ed's experience makes?
6. Why is it so difficult for us to live, fully and responsibly, in the present moment?

7. Which is worse: living in the past or living in the future? What are the pitfalls of each?

## The Fatstock Show (pp. 69–70)

1. Do you see as many similarities as the young man did between a fatstock show and a beauty contest, or do you find the comparison unfair? Explain your answer.
2. What is the purpose of a fatstock show? Of a beauty contest? Do the purposes have any similarity? If so, what does this say about our national attitude toward female beauty?
3. Are there any ways in which being lauded as a "perfect specimen of feminine pulchritude" might have negative effects upon a woman?
4. What does society do with the winners of beauty contests? How about twenty years later? How does it feel to grow old to a woman treasured for her beauty?
5. What do you think of the young man's suspicion that becoming a beauty queen would be the destruction of the winner?
6. Why do newspapers and magazines ask beauty contest winners what they think about world issues?
7. When our society gives such recognition and prizes to those who have physical beauty, what does that say to those born without such beauty, to the deformed, or to those whose beauty is not so visible?
8. How would you set up a national contest for "inner beauty"? What would you tell the judges to look for or to be aware of?
9. If the accident of birth had made you unnaturally handsome or beautiful, would you enter such contests? Why or why not?
10. Can you explain why many women in business and professional life today are made uncomfortable or even hostile by repeated references to their physical appearance, even when the comments are complimentary?

## The Man Who Feared His Neighbors (pp. 71–72)

1. Do you suppose that very many of the millions who have moved in the past generation from farms and small towns to the cities feel apprehensive as this man did? Of what?
2. What factors might influence whether a man responds to his neighbors in friendliness or fear? Which of these factors are caused by his neighbors, and which by him?
3. Do you think that detailed reports in the mass media might tend to

cause crimes to be imitated by other persons? If so, what might be a solution to this problem?

4. When you read or hear of such a crime, what do you usually suspect is the motivation? Do you ever suspect that fear may be the motivation?

5. What is the relationship between the man's extreme fear that others would harm his family and his harming them himself? Should such fears be seen by others as danger signals possibly requiring some psychiatric help?

6. What kind of preventative measures might mental health or even church organizations take to detect and help such persons before they commit tragic acts?

7. How might you have ministered to this man, had he been your next-door neighbor?

8. Should lethal weapons be as readily available to persons as they are? How can a dealer tell who will use them wisely, and who insanely? What kinds of controls would you propose, if any, upon weapon sales?

9. What factors other than the mass media can increase a sense of paranoia about victimization by criminals?

10. Do you think that the message of the Church increases or decreases that paranoia today? Does the Church sometimes unwittingly increase the problem through use of "scare tactics"?


## Too Much, Too Little, Too Late (pp. 73–74)

1. The usual question of course is, How can anyone who lives in an affluent society like ours ever feel unhappy or deprived about anything? But Flora, Mrs. Foster, and Jimmy probably *feel* their own "tragedies" quite as deeply as Mei-Li and Marebi-Gabo feel theirs (perhaps more). Do you think that knowing the problems of Mei-Li or Marebi-Gabo would make Flora, Mrs. Foster, or Jimmy stop feeling sorry for themselves and rejoice in their conditions?

2. How would you answer Flora's plea?

3. If you were standing next to Mrs. Foster at the checkout counter now, would you say anything to her? What?

4. If you were Jimmy's friend, what would you say to him about the motor bike?

5. As a Christian, what would you have to say to Mei-Li or to Marebi-Gabo? Would it really help them?

6. Sickness, malnutrition, and starvation are some of the outward, obvious problems of poverty. What are some of its less obvious, inward problems—what it does to the minds and wills of the poor?

7. Are there inward problems that are caused by living in conditions of affluence? If so, what are some of them? What about the old Christian belief that poverty is a healthier environment for the spirit than affluence?

8. How is Marebi-Gabo different from the others in his response to his outward conditions? We often assume that outward conditions force a person to react in certain predictable ways. Is this true, or does each of us still have a choice of how he will respond, even to tragedy?

9. How is it that the same tragic circumstances seem to destroy and embitter one person while they seem to strengthen and purify another?


## Better to Have Loved? (pp. 75–76)

1. How would you explain to the older brother why people go on loving and befriending, even after betrayal and loss?

2. Have you known persons like the older brother who, having been hurt "once too often," have withdrawn from all possible future relationships except the most superficial? How does their life seem to you? What might encourage them to open up again?

3. What makes for "fullness of life"? If it is the number and depth of human relationships, what happens to those who prefer the "security" of isolation?

4. Is there always the element of risk when we love or befriend another?

5. What, if any, are the differences between the current cultural meanings of love and what the Bible means by the same word?

6. Do you think that the pain of loneliness and isolation is worse, or better, than the pain of many broken relationships? Is there any way to avoid one pain or the other in one's lifetime?

7. Even if the younger brother and his wife do argue and give each other a hard time, does that mean that their marriage is worthless and all bad?

8. Have you ever known the parents of a retarded child? Were they bitter and complaining or all the stronger and more loving for their challenge? How would you explain this?

9. What do you think of the old adage, "Better to have loved and lost, than never to have loved at all"?

## The Hidden Treasure/The Pearl (p. 77)

1. How do you interpret the "treasure" parable as it relates to your own life?
2. Is the proper question for this parable: "What is the treasure?" or "How do I, too, attain such singleness of purpose?"
3. What is Jesus telling us the Kingdom of heaven is like? How is he saying one enters that Kingdom?

## The Unprepared Servant (pp. 77–78)

1. Is the main point of this parable about responsibility or about reward/punishment?
2. The servant in the parable was told by his master—very clearly and precisely—what to do in order to be faithful. Do *you* have a clear and precise grasp of what *you* must do to be a faithful and wise servant? What is it?
3. Why did Jesus insert the element of unexpectedness into this parable? Can you remember other parables in which this element was present? Why is it so important?

## The Rich Fool (p. 78)

1. If the foolish rich man had known that his life was to have ended that night, what might he have done or thought differently?
2. Are we essentially any different from that man when we say, "Tomorrow I will do thus-and-so" or "Next week I'll do such-and-such," or when we have money-making as our sole concern?
3. Why did Jesus refuse to judge upon the question of property rights with the man in the crowd?

## The Rich Man and Lazarus (pp. 78–79)

1. There are at least three possible interpretations of the main point of this parable: (a) that we should always help the needy; (b) that the rich have it good in this life, but the poor will have it good in the next life; or (c) that it is hard for complacent people to hear the truth. Which do you think is the central point?
2. How does this parable apply to your existence? How does it apply to the existence of your church?

**The Gold Coins** (pp. 79–80)

1. Compare and/or contrast this parable with the one about the unprepared servant (pp. 77–78). Do they make the same, or different, points?
2. What is *your* "gold"? How much were you given?
3. To which of the servants would you compare your own stewardship of your "gold" so far in your life?